Stephen Flower

Guide to Promotion

Lectures on Fortification, Military Law, Tactics, Military Topography, and Military Bridges

Stephen Flower

Guide to Promotion
Lectures on Fortification, Military Law, Tactics, Military Topography, and Military Bridges

ISBN/EAN: 9783337267292

Printed in Europe, USA, Canada, Australia, Japan

Cover: Foto ©Paul-Georg Meister /pixelio.de

More available books at **www.hansebooks.com**

GUIDE TO PROMOTION:

OR,

LECTURES ON FORTIFICATION,

MILITARY LAW, TACTICS, MILITARY TOPOGRAPHY, AND

MILITARY BRIDGES.

BY

MAJOR FLOWER,

ROYAL IRISH RIFLES; GARRISON INSTRUCTOR, FERMOY;
LATE DEPUTY ASSISTANT ADJUTANT-GENERAL, CAPE OF GOOD HOPE.

LONDON:
WILLIAM CLOWES AND SONS, LIMITED,
13, CHARING CROSS.
1883.

PREFACE.

THESE lectures are now published at the request of many of my friends, and are intended to be useful not only to officers in preparing for their examinations for promotion, but also to officers of the Militia and others competing for commissions in the Army, and to officers generally who take an interest in their profession, but who for various reasons have not had full opportunity of studying these matters.

The endeavour has been to make them as concise as possible, and at the same time not to leave out anything of importance, or anything contained in the prescribed syllabus.

FERMOY, *November* 1883.

CONTENTS.

FORTIFICATION.

Lecture		Page
I.	Hasty Intrenchments	1
II.	Improvised Field Defences	4
III.	Obstacles	7
IV.	Revetments	12
V.	Artillery	15
VI.	Field Works	19
VII.	Field Works	23
VIII.	Field Works	28
IX.	Defilade of Field Works	31
X.	Details of Field Works	34
XI.	Defence and Attack of Houses	37
XII.	Defence and Attack of Villages, Positions, Woods, and Bridges	41

TACTICS.

I.	The General Functions of the Three Arms	48
II.	Space and Time Required for Troops	51
III.	Advanced Guards	54
IV.	Rear-Guards	58
V.	Outposts	61
VI.	Reconnaissance of the Enemy	66
VII.	Marches	71
VIII.	Infantry	74
IX.	Cavalry	77
X.	Artillery	80
XI.	The Three Arms Combined in Attack	83
XII.	The Three Arms Combined in Defence	86

MILITARY LAW.

Lecture		Page
I.	The Army Act—Crimes and Punishments	90
II.	The Army Act—Courts-Martial	97
III.	The Army Act—Miscellaneous	104
IV.	The Army Act—Miscellaneous	111
V.	The Army Act—Enlistment	116
VI.	The Army Act—Billeting, and Impressment of Carriages	120
VII.	Forfeiture of Pay, Deferred Pay, Good Conduct Pay, Service towards Pension and Medals, &c., by Royal Warrant	123
VIII.	The Rules of Procedure	127
IX.	The Rules of Evidence	130
X.	The Militia Act	136
XI.	The Reserve Forces Act	140

Military Topography	144
Topographical Reconnaissance	148
Military Bridges	152

GUIDE TO PROMOTION.

FIELD FORTIFICATION.

LECTURE I.

HASTY INTRENCHMENTS.

THE object of field fortification is to construct temporary defensive works to enable a force to resist with advantage the attack of a superior force.

There are two descriptions of field fortification, namely, "Hasty," from one to six hours: example, Rorke's Drift; and "Deliberate," from three to fourteen days: example, Plevna.

Principles.—The four great principles of all fortification are: 1st. Cover for the defenders from view and fire. 2nd. No cover for the enemy from view and fire. 3rd. The enemy's approach to be made as difficult as possible. 4th. Freedom of movement for the defenders.

Parapets, ditches, and obstacles are the main elements of field fortification. The parapet covers the defenders from view and fire. The ditch furnishes the earth for the parapet. The ditch and the obstacles in it and in front of it obstruct the progress of the enemy. All cover within effective range of the parapet should be destroyed.

Technical Terms.—A "salient angle" is one projecting outwards. A "re-entering angle" is one receding inwards. "The capital" is a line bisecting a salient angle. The "gorge" is a line joining the inner extremities of an open work. The straight lines of parapet inclosing a work are called "faces." A "flank" is a line of parapet intended to defend another line by flanking fire. A "line of defence" is the distance from a flank to the furthest point flanked by it. The angle formed by a flank and a line of defence is termed the "angle of defence."

Penetration of Musketry.—From experiments made with the Martini-Henry rifle, with service ammunition, and at twenty yards range, its penetration was found to be,

In a parapet of unrammed earth	18 to 21 inches.
In brushwood gabions filled with earth	18 to 20 ,,
In a parapet of sand	15 to 18 ,,
In sandbags filled with earth	9 to 12 ,,

Shelter Trenches.—The quickest and most convenient method of obtaining cover for troops in the field is by "shelter trenches."

There are three kinds, and they are called respectively "the half-hour," "the one-hour," and the "two-hours" shelter trenches, from the time taken to construct them. All are 18 inches deep, with a berm of 18 inches, and a parapet 18 inches high. Their width is the only thing in which they differ; the half-hour shelter trench is $2\frac{1}{2}$ feet wide; the one-hour trench is 5 feet, and the two-hour trench is 8 feet wide. The half-hour trench gives room for one rank kneeling, the one-hour trench for two ranks kneeling, and the two-hour trench for two ranks and the supernumerary rank kneeling.

In executing a line of shelter trench the diggers are stationed at intervals of 5 feet.

A "shelter pit" affording cover for a man on outpost duty can be made in five minutes.

A "charger pit" to protect a horse can be made by three men in two hours; depth 3 feet and parapet 3 feet high.

Gun Pits and Gun Epaulments.—There are two methods of obtaining hasty cover for field guns: namely, "gun pits" and "gun epaulments."

In the former the gun stands in a wide trench, the earth from which forms the parapet; through a rough embrasure in the parapet the gun fires. This is the quickest method. In the latter the gun stands on the natural surface of the ground, trenches being dug in front and at each side of it to cover the gunners; the earth from these trenches and from a ditch in front forms a bank or epaulment to cover the gun. The gun fires over the top of the epaulment. This method gives a harder surface for the wheels of the gun to stand on, and the epaulment can sometimes be made whilst the gun is in action.

Rifle Pits.—" Rifle pits " are often used during siege operations, and in front of the siege works, and from them the enemy's gunners can be picked off through their embrasures. One man with a pick and shovel can dig a rifle pit 4 feet deep and 4 feet in diameter, with a step to get in and out by, in one hour. A loophole is made of four sand-bags filled with earth. Rifle pits are usually made at night and occupied by day; they may afterwards be connected by a narrow trench three or four feet deep.

LECTURE II.

IMPROVISED FIELD DEFENCES.

Hedges.—Hedges afford cover from view, but not from fire unless well banked up with earth. Very often there is a ditch in connection with a hedge, which if on the enemy's side will serve as an obstacle, and if on the defenders' side as a trench to fire from. In either case, the ditch may, if necessary, and time and means permit, be enlarged, and the earth banked up against the hedge. If there is no ditch already on the defenders' side a trench may be dug, and the earth banked up against the hedge to strengthen it.

Sometimes a banquette will be necessary to fire over a high and thick hedge.

Walls.—A wall properly prepared makes a very good parapet against musketry or shrapnel shell, but will not resist common shell. If it is less than 4 feet high men may kneel and fire over it. If 4 or 5 feet high they may stand and fire over it. If 6 feet high it should be loopholed $4\frac{1}{2}$ feet from the ground, or it may be notched down from the top by crowbars, or men may fire over it from a banquette 18 inches high. The loopholes should in either case be 1 yard apart. A 10 or 12-foot wall might have two tiers of loopholes; a banquette of some kind, for example, one of planks supported on casks, would be necessary for the upper tier.

If time and means permit, small ditches may be dug in front of a wall, or small trenches in rear of it, and the earth piled up against the wall to strengthen it.

Logs of wood supported on stones laid on the top of a wall will afford good head cover for men firing over it, or sand-bag loopholes will answer the same purpose.

Embankments and Cuttings.—Embankments and cuttings parallel to the front afford good cover to the supports and reserves; but if they have to be occupied for defence by the shooting line they can if necessary, and time and means permit, be quickly prepared in several ways.

In most cases a small "shelter trench" constructed according to circumstances, and taking into consideration the slope of the ground and the nature of the embankment or cutting, will best answer the purpose.

Roads.—Roads have usually hedges, walls, or banks in connection with them which could be prepared for defence. But if necessary, shelter trenches can be constructed parallel to the road or across it. If the enemy is expected to approach by the road itself, it should be enfiladed for as great a distance as possible by field-guns from "gun pits" and "gun epaulments" and large quantities of abatis should be placed across the road under fire of the guns; whilst infantry in shelter trenches would be able to bring a flanking fire on the enemy as he approached the abatis.

Stockades.—A stockade is a rough timber parapet, consisting of squared logs of wood 10 feet long and 18 inches square, sunk 3 feet in the ground and standing, therefore, 7 feet above it. The logs should touch each other, and be secured near the top inside by spiking a stout ribband of wood to them.

Loopholes should be cut in the joints and before the timbers are placed in position. The loopholes should be 1 yard apart and 6 feet above the ground, the defenders standing on a banquette 18 inches high to fire from them. A small ditch may be dug outside, and the earth from it piled up on a berm against the stockade as high as the loopholes, to give additional strength.

Stockades are used when timber is plentiful, and artillery fire is not expected.

Tambours.—Tambours are formed of stockade work, and are sometimes roofed over like a blockhouse; their usual shape is rectangular or triangular. They are useful to cover an entrance, and for flanking stockades, walls, &c., and are pierced with loopholes for as many men as can conveniently use them. The usual position for a tambour is covering a gate or entrance. If a square or rectangular inclosure had to be flanked, tambours at two of the opposite salient angles would be sufficient, and rough openings might be made in the angles for retreat.

LECTURE III.

OBSTACLES.

OBSTACLES are chiefly used in connection with field works, and are intended to check the progress of an enemy advancing to the assault, and cause him to move slowly and in disorder under the close and effective musketry fire of the defenders.

They are usually placed beyond the ditch, but sometimes in the ditch itself, or on the berm, and should fulfil the following conditions, namely:—

They should be situated under the effective musketry fire of the defenders, and should not be exposed to the enemy's artillery fire; they should not afford any cover to the enemy, and should cause him time and difficulty to surmount, or remove, and should be so arranged as not to interfere with any advance or counter attack on the part of the defenders.

Obstacles are either natural or artificial. Precipices, swamps, water, &c., are natural obstacles; palisades, fraises, chevaux-de-frise, abatis, small and large trous de loup, entanglements, stakes, crowsfeet, barricades, &c., are artificial obstacles.

Palisades.—Palisades are stout triangular palings, 10 feet long, and pointed at the top, each side of the triangle being about 8 inches. They are firmly secured to ribbands near both top and bottom, and are placed upright, or slightly sloping in a trench 3 feet deep. The palisades are 3 or 4 inches apart; the top ribband should not be on the enemy's side, and should be nailed on after the palisades are fixed in position. Palisades are generally placed either in the ditch, or to close the gorge of a work, or other concealed position.

Fraises.—Fraises are palisades planted horizontally or nearly so in the ground, with the ridges uppermost; they are spiked to two ribbands of wood near their butts, one ribband being above and the other below; the butts of the fraises and both ribbands are buried about 5 feet in the ground. Fraises are usually placed in the slope of escarp and counterscarp; if the former, they should slope downwards, but if the latter, upwards.

Chevaux-de-frise.—Chevaux-de-frise are articles of store, and are made in lengths of 6 feet; each length consists of a hollow iron tube with holes through it at intervals for the spears, which are 12 in number, 6 feet long, and cross each other at right angles. In placing this obstacle in position, the "slotted" holes for the spears should be downwards or the spears might be drawn out, and the lengths ought to be chained together. For travelling, the spears are packed inside the hollow tubes.

Chevaux-de-frise can be improvised with beams of wood, and iron railings, or pointed stakes, &c. They form a good temporary barrier across a road, or street, or at the entrance of a work.

Abatis.—Abatis consists of small trees, or large branches of trees laid close together, the butts firmly secured, being buried, or staked to the ground; the branches, trimmed and pointed, being turned towards the enemy. Hard and tough woods are best: the branches should stand at least as high as a man's breast. It is one of the best obstacles, and is usually placed beyond the ditch, in a trench dug on purpose for it, the earth from which forms a glacis for its protection; it may also be placed upright in the ditch itself. On account of the labour of cutting and dragging it from a distance, it is seldom used unless trees are plentiful and near at hand.

Military Pits.—Military pits, or "trous de loup," are holes with a sharp-pointed stake fixed in them, and are of two kinds, deep and shallow. The deep ones are 6 feet deep, and in shape like an inverted cone, and are 6 feet in diameter at top and 1 foot at bottom. The shallow pits are $2\frac{1}{2}$ feet deep, and in shape like an inverted square pyramid, being 3 feet square at top. Military pits should never be made between $2\frac{1}{2}$ and 6 feet deep, or they might serve the enemy for rifle pits. The points of the stakes should be level with the ground. A man can dig ten shallow pits, or one and a half deep ones, in a day of eight hours. The deep ones are 10 feet from centre to centre, and the excavated earth is piled up in the intervals. The shallow ones touch each other, and the excavated earth is thrown to the front as a glacis. Both kinds are a good obstacle against cavalry, and are made in several chequered rows, usually opposite the salient angles, beyond the counterscarp.

Entanglements.—A brushwood entanglement is formed by cutting the stems of trees, bushes, vines, &c., half through, about 3 feet from the ground, and then bending down the tops to the ground and securing them there by pickets.

A wire entanglement consists of several rows of stakes placed chequerwise 6 feet apart, and connected by stout wire, twisted round their tops, about 12 or 18 inches from the ground.

The bands of Jones's iron gabion being buttoned

and connected together and placed in rows, make a good entanglement. Entanglements are often used in connection with military pits; they are quickly made, difficult to destroy, and impassable by cavalry.

Stakes.—Pointed stakes can be quickly made and placed, and are very useful on the berm, in the ditch, between military pits, and beyond the counterscarp; the points of the stakes should project 1 or 2 feet above the ground.

Crowsfeet.—Crowsfeet consist of four iron spikes $2\frac{1}{2}$ or 3 inches long, welded together at their heads, so that, however thrown, one point is uppermost. They are very useful against cavalry, and should be placed on open ground, and in fords, &c.

Barricades.—Barricades may be made of whatever there is at hand, such as carts, and casks, filled with stones or earth, timber, furniture, bales of wool, waggons, &c. They are usually formed across a road or street, or to defend a bridge, &c., and may have a banquette on which the defenders stand and fire. Barricades are often arranged one behind the other, and the means of retreat through a barricade should be provided for, and the front of the barricade should be flanked.

Miscellaneous Obstacles.—Harrows, broken wheels, rough stones, broken bottles, &c., in fact whatever there is available, should always be turned to account.

Surmounting Obstacles.—Abatis may be cut with

axes and drawn away with ropes. Palisades and fraises may be cut down with axes or blown in with powder or guncotton. Entanglements and military pits can be crossed by a temporary roadway of doors, planks, hurdles, &c. A ditch may be partially filled up with bundles of hay or straw, bales of wool, fascines, &c. Chevaux-de-frise may be rolled over to one side. The above operations, however, are impossible under heavy fire.

LECTURE IV.

REVETMENTS.

A "REVETMENT" is any support which enables the earth to stand at a steeper slope than it naturally would, which is with a base equal to its height or $\frac{1}{4}$.

The most common revetments are gabions, fascines, sand-bags, sods, plants, and hurdles.

Gabions.—Gabions are strong cylindrical baskets, open at both ends, 3 feet high, and 2 feet in diameter when finished. They are made by placing ten pickets $3\frac{1}{2}$ feet long, upright in the ground, in a circle of $10\frac{1}{2}$ inches radius, and at equal distance apart, and then weaving brushwood in and out of them in a particular way called "waling." Pairing rods are then put on at each end, and are sewn to the webwork by four "withes," or by wire, or spun yarn. A gabion can be made by three men in two hours. They support the earth at a slope of $\frac{4}{1}$. These brushwood gabions are perishable, and require much time and labour to make, so that iron gabions are now a good deal used, and are articles of store, such as Jones's iron band gabions, Tyler's sheet-iron gabions, and Smith's wire-net gabions. Gabions when placed in revetment are filled with earth, and are laid in alternate rows with fascines; the bottom row being fascines and the top row gabions.

Fascines.—Fascines are strong faggots of brushwood, 18 feet long and 9 inches in diameter.

To make them, a "cradle" must first be made of five pairs of trestles, 4 feet apart, and correctly dressed in a line; brushwood is then laid on the cradle, and compressed by an iron chain called a "choker," to the proper diameter; they are then bound tightly at intervals of 18 inches with "withes" of brushwood; or with wire, or spun yarn; they are then trimmed with a knife and the ends sawn off square. A fascine can be made by five men in one hour; they support the earth at a slope of $\frac{4}{1}$; the bottom row is laid in a groove 3 inches deep. Fascines are secured in their places in revetment by pickets, or anchoring pickets, $3\frac{1}{2}$ feet long. If shorter fascines are required, they can be sawn off to any length.

Sand-bags.—Sand-bags are made of canvas, and if tarred over are fairly durable; when empty and laid flat they are 32 inches long and 16 inches wide. They hold a bushel of earth, but should only be three-quarters full for convenience of building.

In building them up into revetment, they should be laid in alternate courses of "headers" and "stretchers," and with the joints broken, the stretchers being parallel to the parapet, and the necks of the headers towards the parapet. When built up they occupy a space of 20 inches long, 10 inches wide, and 6 inches high.

Sods. — Sods are usually cut 18 inches long, 9 inches wide, and $4\frac{1}{2}$ inches thick. In building them up into revetment, they are flattened down, however, to a thickness of 3 inches. Sods should also be laid in alternate rows of headers and stretchers, and with the joints broken and grass downwards. They form a neat and durable revetment, and support the earth at a slope of $\frac{3}{1}$. Two builders should lay from 70 to 100 sods an hour.

Casks.—Casks filled with earth form a good revetment; but should not be exposed to fire on account of the splinters from them.

Planks. — Planks form a good revetment, and should be secured in their places by stakes.

Hurdles.—Common sheep hurdles are sometimes available, but if not, can either be made, or a continuous hurdle revetment constructed in the position it is to occupy. Hurdles make a good revetment; they are made much in the same way as gabions, but in a curve, which is afterwards straightened. They are kept in their places by stakes, and by securing their tops to the parapet by anchoring pickets.

LECTURE V.

ARTILLERY.

Field Guns.—All the field guns now in our service are muzzle-loaders, which are simpler, cheaper, stronger, more quickly loaded, and less liable to get out of order than breech-loaders.

They comprise the seven, nine, thirteen, and sixteen-pounders. The seven-pounders are used for rough or mountainous country, and are usually carried by mules on pack-saddles; the nine-pounders for light field batteries and horse artillery; the thirteen and sixteen-pounders for heavy field batteries. In addition to these, there is the gatling, which is a machine-gun having ten rifled barrels; it is loaded and fired by means of a breech handle, five men being required to serve it; it can fire from 300 to 400 rounds per minute, and is used to most advantage in defending streets, roads, and all narrow places, such as bridges and defiles.

Parapets to resist artillery.—The thickness of an earthen parapet to resist artillery should be about

1½ times the penetration of the projectiles used against it.

To resist the	gatling	it should be	3 feet.
,,	7-pounder	,,	6 to 9 ,,
,,	9-pounder	,,	9 to 12 ,,
,,	13 and 16-pounder	,,	15 to 18 ,,

Artillery Fire.—Artillery fire, with reference to the horizontal plane, is said to be either frontal, oblique, enfilade, or reverse.

Frontal fire is that which strikes perpendicularly or nearly so to the line of the object aimed at.

Reverse fire strikes the object in rear.

Oblique fire strikes the object in front, but not perpendicularly.

Enfilade fire is that directed along a certain line, the gun being in prolongation of that line.

Artillery fire with reference to its trajectory may be direct, curved or indirect, or high angle.

Direct fire means fire with the service charge not exceeding 15° elevation.

Indirect or curved fire means fire with reduced charges not exceeding 15° elevation.

High angle fire means with an elevation exceeding 15° and with any charge.

When guns fire at an object much below them, the fire is said to be plunging, but when the projectile sweeps the surface of the ground, the fire is called grazing.

Projectiles.—The projectiles fired from field guns are common shell, shrapnel shell, and case shot.

A common shell is a hollow cast-iron projectile filled with a bursting charge of powder; its shape is that of a cylinder with a pointed head, its length is about three times its diameter, the bursting charge is ignited by a percussion fuze fixed in the head of the shell. Common shell are used against artillery or against masses of troops at long ranges, especially if in column or under cover, and against field works, buildings, &c.; the effective range extends up to between 3000 and 4000 yards.

A shrapnel shell is a little shorter than a common shell, but is similar in shape and outside appearance, and is distinguished from it by its head being painted red. Its interior is filled with round bullets imbedded in resin. A small bursting charge is placed at the base; and a time-fuze is fitted to its head, communicating with the bursting charge by a tube and primer. The fuze at the proper moment ignites the bursting charge, the thin crust of the shrapnel bursts, and the bullets, being set free, spread out and are carried forward. Shrapnel are used against troops in extended order, and on open level ground; its extreme range is about 3000 yards.

A case-shot is a tin cylinder filled with round bullets mixed with clay and sand; it bursts in the bore of the gun and the bullets are scattered at the muzzle. It is very effective at short ranges from 100 to 300 yards and can be used up to 400 yards.

Fuzes.—The time-fuze is tapering in shape and is

made of beech-wood; its interior is filled with fuze composition; the figures printed on a time-fuze indicate the number of seconds the composition takes to burn to each point. Before fitting the fuze to the shell, it is bored by a gimlet for the estimated range in seconds; the discharge of the gun ignites the fuze, and when the composition has burnt as far as the hole which was bored, the flame rushes out of the fuze into the bursting charge and the shell bursts.

The percussion fuze is made of gun-metal and its construction is rather complicated, and there is a double action. The discharge of the gun sets the percussion arrangement free to act, and the shock of the projectile striking an object ignites the fuze.

Cartridges and Tubes.—Guns are fired by means of metal tubes, filled with composition and fixed in the vent of the gun. The copper friction-tube is generally used; it is about 3 inches long, and has a small ring at the top. To fire the gun a small cord is hooked on to the ring and pulled with a jerk. Cartridges are made up in silk bags, and contain charges of Rifled Large Grain powder (marked RLG), the grains of which are of about the same size as grains of barley; the weight of the charge is about one-fifth the weight of the projectile.

LECTURE VI.

FIELD WORKS.

Tracing.—In throwing up field works, the first thing to be decided upon is the shape and size of the work, also the command, thickness of parapet, and dimensions of the ditch. The magistral line (or outline) is then traced by tapes, pickets being driven in at every angle, and the tape passed round the pickets. The outline should be proportioned to the number of men, and guns, for which the work is built; at the rate of 1 yard per file, and 5 yards per gun, the parapet should be so adapted to the ground, that every spot within range is under fire; there should be mutual defence between all the parts of a work, which means that the ground should be swept by both direct and flanking fire. The long lines of parapet should be secure from enfilade fire. Re-entering angles should be from 90 to 100 degrees; salient angles as obtuse as possible but never less than 60 degrees. Flanks should not be less than 12 yards long. The lines of defence should not exceed the effective range of musketry; generally speaking, this can be taken at from 300 to 400 yards, beyond which distance it has been found that a steady and well-sustained fire cannot be depended upon during a siege.

Laying-off angles on the ground.—The best method

of laying-off angles on the ground, if there is no "field level" available, is to drive a picket into the ground, where the angle is to be, and then to stretch a line for the capital; then with the picket as a centre and with 57 inches radius describe an arc cutting the capital; on this arc with a tape measure off as many inches as there are to be degrees in the angle, join the two points to the picket, and the required angle is formed. The reason for taking a radius of 57 is that $57 \times 2\pi = 360$; and the circumference of a circle $= 2\pi r$.

Profiling.—After the magistral line has been traced, profiles of wood are set up at right angles to the parapet, so that the workmen may see what the exact shape of the work is to be when finished. There should be at least two profiles to each line of parapet, but if the faces are long, profiles should be at intervals of 20 feet. At the angles there should be oblique profiles.

Technical Terms.—The "terreplein" is the surface of the ground inside a work. The "plane of site" is a plane tangent to the ground on which the work is built. The "command" is the height of the interior crest above the plane of sight. The "relief" is the height of the interior crest above the bottom of the ditch.

Parapet.—The parapet consists of slope of banquette, banquette, interior slope, superior slope, and exterior slope. A berm separates the parapet from the ditch. The ditch consists of escarp, bottom of ditch, and counterscarp. A glacis is often formed beyond the ditch. The usual dimensions of a parapet are:—slope of banquette $\frac{1}{2}$; banquette 3 feet for single rank, and $4\frac{1}{2}$ feet for double rank; interior slope $\frac{4}{1}$; command 8 feet on level ground; it varies from 6 to 12 feet; if less than 6 it does not afford sufficient cover, if more than 12 the labour of construction is very great; thickness of parapet from 6 to 18 feet or $1\frac{1}{2}$ times the penetration of the projectiles likely to be used against it; supeiror slope from $\frac{1}{6}$ to $\frac{1}{4}$, exterior slope $\frac{1}{1}$; berm from 1 to 6 feet; ditch from 6 to 12 feet deep, and not less than 12 feet wide at top; escarp $\frac{2}{1}$, counterscarp $\frac{3}{1}$. If the ditch is less than 6 feet deep or 12 feet wide it is not an efficient obstacle; if more than 12 feet deep the labour of excavation is very great.

Working Parties.—After the profiles are set up, the inner and outer lines of the parapet, and also the top of escarp and counterscarp are "spitlocked" or marked with a pickaxe. The working party is then told off into diggers, shovellers, and rammers. To every three diggers there should be two shovellers and one rammer. The diggers, shovellers, and rammers are then placed and set to work. The diggers, 5 feet apart, excavate the ditch with picks and shovels, commencing on the escarp, and throw the earth 12 feet inwards to the shovellers who level it; the rammers walk about and ram the earth down firmly. The ditch is usually dug in successive depths of 3 feet, the sides being left in steps which are afterwards scarped away.

Two rows of diggers are sometimes employed for very wide ditches, and should then be arranged so as not to interfere with each other. If there is also to be a trench, one row of diggers would excavate the ditch and another row the trench, and they would throw the earth towards each other. In average soil 1 cubic yard per hour is considered fair for an untrained workman. A surplus of earth will exist at the salients, and a deficit at re-entering angles. This may be rectified by throwing it obliquely towards the re-entering angles, or using it for a glacis. Drains should be made at the same time as the parapet, leading from the work under the parapet into the ditch.

A company of sixty men would be told off as a working party into thirty diggers, twenty shovellers, and ten rammers. They would excavate a ditch 50 yards long at the rate of 120 cubic yards, in a relief of four hours.

LECTURE VII.

FIELD WORKS.

The size of the ditch of an earthwork is determined by the quantity of earth required to build the parapet. The depth of the ditch varies from 6 to 12 feet and its width at top should not be less than 12 feet. It is usual to assume the depth, and to calculate the width in the following manner. As the area of the profile of a parapet is equal to the area of the profile of the ditch, the former is first formed by measuring the two triangles and two trapezoids of which every parapet consists. Supposing this to be 120 square feet, then the area of the profile of the ditch will also be 120 square feet. Assuming that the ditch is to be 10 feet deep, $\frac{120}{10} = 12$ feet = mean width of ditch. The mean width $+ \frac{1}{2}$ sum of the bases of escarp and counterscarp = width of ditch at top, and the mean width $- \frac{1}{2}$ sum of the bases of escarp and counterscarp = width of ditch at bottom.

Example of calculating the width of ditch for a parapet 8 feet high and 12 feet thick, with the usual slopes; the depth of ditch being 10 feet, slope of escarp $\frac{2}{1}$, slope of counterscarp $\frac{3}{1}$:—

24   FIELD FORTIFICATION.

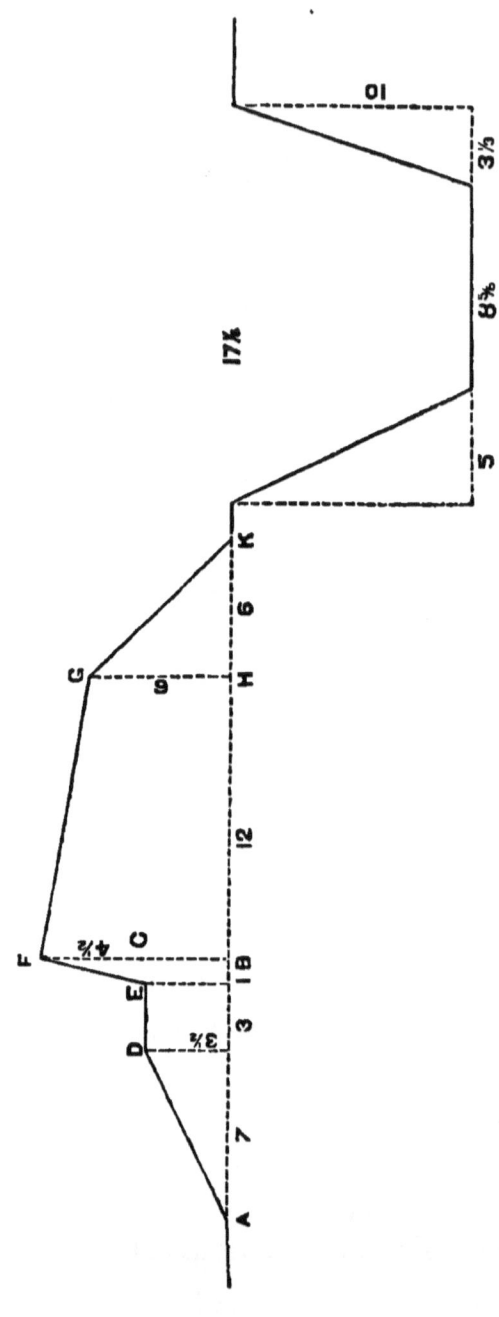

The area of the above parapet

$$= ABCD + ECF + FBHG + GHK$$

$ABCD = \dfrac{4+11}{2} \times 3\frac{1}{2} = \dfrac{15}{2} \times \dfrac{7}{2} = \dfrac{105}{4} = 26\frac{1}{4}$ square feet.

$ECF = \frac{1}{2} \times 4\frac{1}{2} = \dfrac{9}{4}$ $\qquad\qquad = 2\frac{1}{4}$,,

$FBHG = \dfrac{8+6}{2} \times 12 = 7 \times 12$ $\quad = 84$,,

$GHK = \dfrac{6 \times 6}{2}$ $\qquad\qquad\qquad = 18$,,

$\qquad\qquad\qquad\qquad\qquad\overline{\qquad\qquad}$
$\qquad\qquad\qquad\qquad\qquad 130\frac{1}{2}$ = Area of ditch.

$\dfrac{130\frac{1}{2}}{10} = 13$ feet, mean width of ditch.

Half the sum of the bases of escarp and counterscarp is $4\frac{1}{8}$ feet.

Therefore $13 + 4\frac{1}{8} = 17\frac{1}{8}$ feet = width of ditch at top.
$\qquad\quad 13 - 4\frac{1}{8} = 8\frac{7}{8}$,, = ,, bottom.

Deblai and remblai are terms used to express the earth before and after excavation. The latter generally exceeds the former by $\frac{1}{10}$, but in practice it is not necessary to make any allowance, but to use the excess for a glacis and the re-entering angles.

There are two kinds of field works, namely, open works and closed works. Open works are those whose parapets do not entirely surround the site occupied, such as Redans and Lunettes. Closed works are those whose parapets entirely surround the site occupied, such as Redoubts and Forts.

Redans.—A " redan " or " flêche " is an open work

consisting of two faces meeting in a salient angle greater than 60°, the gorge being open. Its defects are that the salient angle, ditches, and gorge are undefended, and there is no flank defence. These defects may be remedied by rounding off the salient angle, or cutting it off so as to form a face 6 yards long, and by adding flanks (not less than 12 yards long) to defend the salient and ditches, and by placing palisades across the gorge.

Lunettes.—A "lunette" is an open work consisting of two faces, meeting in a salient angle of about 120°, and two other faces parallel or nearly so to the capital. These works have the same defects as redans, and they may be remedied in the same manner.

Open works are suitable for advanced positions when their gorges are protected by other works in rear or by some natural obstacle such as a river. They should be seldom used as isolated works, except to cover a guard or picquet, bridge, defile, &c.

Redoubts.—A "redoubt" is a closed work having no re-entering angles and consequently no flank defence; they may be square, rectangular, or polygonal; their defects are that their salients and ditches are undefended, and there is no flank defence. These defects may be remedied by cutting off the salient angles, throwing out auxiliary flanks, and making small works such as caponiers in the ditches to flank them.

Forts.—A "fort" is a closed work having both

salient and re-entering angles, and consequently flank defence. A "star fort" is a work composed of alternate salient and re-entering angles, and is made by tracing equilateral triangles on any polygon. Their defects are numerous, namely, they are difficult to make, have many salient points of attack, their ditches are nearly undefended, the interior space is small, and their faces are much exposed to reverse and enfilade fire.

A "bastion fort" is the most perfect of all field works, having mutual defence between all the parts; their construction however is complicated, and they require much time and labour to make, and a large garrison; they are therefore only used for important positions, and when sufficient time is available.

Closed works are suitable for detached "posts" and for the flanks of an "intrenched position," also for important points in the main line of defence.

Size of Works and Garrisons.—The size of works depends upon the number of men and guns that can be spared for their defence. The distribution is reckoned at one man for every yard of banquette, half that number a few yards in rear as support, and one-quarter of the whole as reserve. Or allow one yard for every two men and five yards for every gun.

For example: if a redoubt had to be thrown up for 200 men and three guns, it should have a crest line of 115 yards, but if the guns were firing " en barbette " no allowance need be made for them, and the crest-line would be 100 yards.

A flank should not be less than 12 yards long for infantry, or 25 yards long for artillery.

As a rule garrisons do not have to live inside a work, but if they had to, 15 square feet must be allowed for every man and 600 square feet for every gun (including gunners, &c.) and 500 square feet for every traverse.

LECTURE VIII.

FIELD WORKS.

Lines. — When several works are combined for mutual support, and for the defence of a certain position, they are called " Lines." If connected together they are called " Continuous Lines," if unconnected, " Lines with intervals."

If lines inclose a space between themselves and a fortified place, the inclosed space is called an " intrenched camp." When lines are intended for an inferior army to defend itself against a superior one without reference to siege operations, they are called an " intrenched position."

Long continuous lines were much used in former days, but lines with intervals are more suited to modern tactics. Short continuous lines are sometimes useful if their flanks are secure.

Continuous Lines. — Continuous lines may be formed of redans joined by curtains, called "redan lines," or of bastion fronts joined together, called "bastion lines," which are, however, seldom used, as their construction is intricate, and they are not easily adapted to the ground; or of faces and flanks alternating, making angles of 90° with each other, called "crémaillère," or indented lines; these are very simple, and especially useful for closing the interval between two strong redoubts or forts.

Lines with intervals.—If a single line is to be made, the works may be 500 yards apart for mutual musketry defence, and a mile apart for mutual artillery defence.

If a double line of works is required, the front line may be of open works; and the rear line, at least 600 yards behind the front line, should consist of closed works covering the intervals.

If a double line of closed works is used, the rear faces of the front line should be slighter and of less command in case the enemy should gain possession of them. In the front line one or more guns should be placed "en barbette" at each salient, and three guns at least in each flank; the heaviest guns should be placed in the rear line, on account of their greater range, and because they would be more secure.

The arrangement of all the works should be such as to defend the works in front and the intervals between them by artillery and musketry fire, sweep the ground in front, enfilade the probable line of advance, and bring a cross fire in front of the salients.

Bridge-heads. — A "bridge-head" is a work or a series of works, usually open at the gorge, such as redans and lunettes, to cover the communication across a river, and consists of the work covering the bridge, advanced works connected with the defence, and batteries on the bank in rear, defending and flanking the above.

The work covering the bridge is usually a blunted lunette, and the advanced works are usually redans.

The principal points in arranging these works are to cover the bridge from the enemy's view and fire, to have a good frontal, flank, and cross fire from the works and batteries, satisfactory means for the defenders to advance or retreat, and that the works in front, and the bridge itself should be commanded by the works and batteries in rear.

The number of works, and their size and armament, will depend upon the importance of the defence and the time and means available.

For bridge-heads, re-entering bends of a river are much the best for defensive purposes; but for the position of a military bridge, straight lines are often preferable, as the depth is less variable and the current less rapid.

LECTURE IX.

DEFILADE OF FIELD WORKS.

DEFILADE means regulating the parapets, trenches, and traverses, so as to cover or screen the defenders from the enemy's view and fire.

On level ground 8 feet may be assumed as sufficient height for a parapet; but if there is commanding ground within 3000 yards of a work, 8 feet will be too low, and the necessary height will be found by a process called "defilading."

The enemy's fire is assumed to be delivered 4½ feet above the ground he stands on, and to be harmless if it passes 8 feet above the terreplein of a work; therefore, if by raising the parapet or by lowering the terreplein you make it impossible for the enemy's fire to pass lower than 8 feet above the terreplein, you have defiladed the work.

To make clear the following process of "defilading" it is

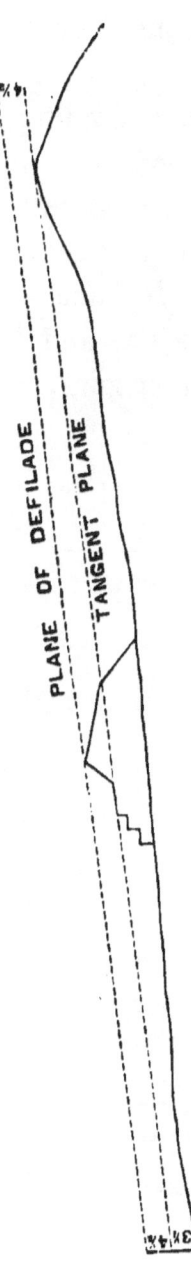

necessary to explain the meaning of the expressions "tangent plane" and "plane of defilade." Tangent plane is an imaginary plane touching the commanding ground, and passing 3½ feet above the gorge of a work. Plane of defilade is an imaginary plane parallel to the tangent plane and 4½ feet above it.

Defilade of Open Works.—Open works, such as redans and lunettes, should be defiladed as far as their gorge as follows:

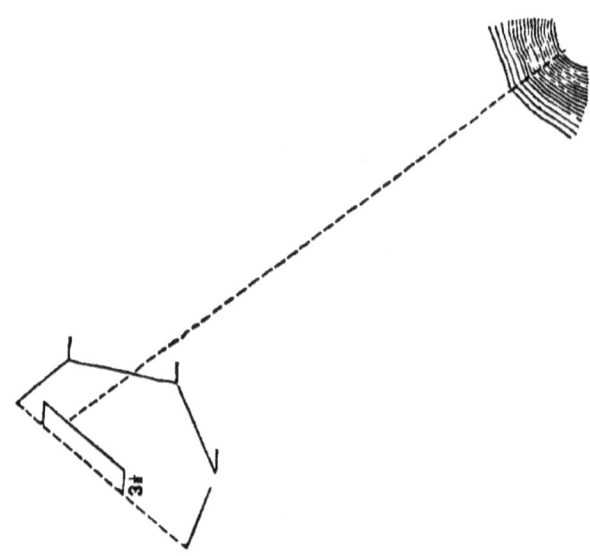

Plant upright poles at all the angles, stretch a rope across the gorge 3½ feet above the ground; observe and mark the points where the tangent plane cuts the poles, and mark the poles again

4½ feet above those points; the upper marks give the necessary height for the parapet.

Defilade of Closed Works.—A closed work such as a redoubt would be defiladed as follows:—

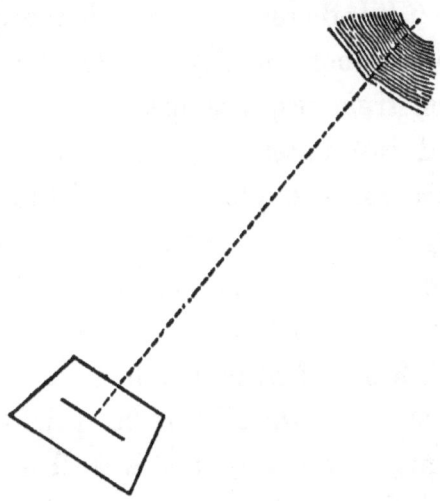

A certain portion of it, say the half nearest the enemy, would be defiladed as above, and the other portion would be defiladed by building a traverse or "parados" across the centre, sufficiently high to cover the defenders of the rear faces from reverse fire.

As the command of a field work should not exceed 12 feet, it will often be better to lower the terreplein than to raise the parapet, and still better to both lower the terreplein and raise the parapet.

No work should be built at all within range of commanding ground if it can be avoided; sometimes, however, it cannot be avoided, and then the long faces should be traced perpendicular to the line of fire, and the work defiladed as above.

D

LECTURE X.

DETAILS OF FIELD WORKS.

Blindages.—" Blindages" are rough temporary constructions of timber, usually sunken, for the protection of guns, trenches, passages, &c., from vertical fire. "Field casemates" are very similar constructions, and are for the protection of the troops not actually engaged at the time. The walls of both are made of stout beams of wood, 12 inches in diameter, and the roof of logs, planks, or fascines, covered with 3 or 4 feet of earth, to make it bomb-proof. A "splinter-proof" can be quickly made by placing beams of wood against a wall or parapet at an angle of about 50°, and serves as a protection against splinters of shells and shrapnel fire.

Caponiers.—A "caponier" is a covered sunken building for the flank defence of a ditch; its walls are of stockade and are loopholed, its roof of timber covered with earth. It is usually made at a salient angle, so as to flank two ditches, and it should extend across the ditch, the counterscarp at that point being widened. The communication with it is by a gallery under the parapet.

Escarp and Counterscarp Galleries.—" Escarp and counterscarp galleries" are constructions of timber, something like caponiers, under the escarp and counter scarp for the flank defence of ditches. The escarp gallery, if made at a re-entering angle, will flank two ditches, and a counterscarp gallery should be made at a salient angle for the same purpose.

They are both loopholed, and there is communication with an escarp gallery by a passage under the parapet, and with a counterscarp gallery by a passage under the parapet and across the ditch.

Traverses.—Traverses are mounds of earth, of the same profile as the parapet, to protect the garrison from enfilade fire. If only 4 feet thick at top they are called "splinter-proofs." If made as a protection from reverse fire, they are called "parados." If made to cover the entrance of a work, they should be long enough to intercept the most oblique fire. If made as a protection from enfilade fire they should be at right angles to the parapet, and sufficiently long to protect the men and guns actually firing. The slopes of a traverse should be $\frac{1}{1}$ on the side exposed to fire, the other side should be revetted to a slope of $\frac{2}{1}$ or $\frac{3}{1}$ to save space.

Entrances and Barriers.—The entrance of a work should be on the side least exposed to fire, and should if possible be flanked. For infantry it should be 4 feet wide, and for artillery 7 feet. It should be revetted, and closed by a pair of heavy timber gates, opening outwards; the ditch is crossed either by a plank bridge, or by leaving a piece of the natural ground opposite the entrance.

Blockhouses.—"Blockhouses" are strong loopholed barracks, usually rectangular; but sometimes in the shape of a cross, for flank defence; and sometimes there are two storeys, the upper one being diagonally over the lower one. The walls are made of stockade, and the roof of timber covered with 3 or 4 feet of earth. The interior should be at least 7 or 8 feet high, and 9 feet wide for one row of beds, and 15 feet for two rows. Outside there is a ditch, the earth from which is piled up against the walls as high as the loopholes, to give additional strength. Blockhouses are much used as isolated posts, in mountainous and well wooded countries, but are of little use when exposed to artillery fire.

Reduits.—A "reduit" is a small work inside a large one, from which to prolong the defence if the large one is taken. A small blockhouse makes a very good reduit, but should be as low as possible, so as not to be exposed to fire; for which reason the floor should be sunken, and the walls only 6 feet high.

Embrasures.—An "embrasure" is an opening made in the parapet for a gun to fire through. The names of its parts are the "sole," the "sill," the "cheeks," the "neck," and the "mouth." Embrasures should be at least 15 feet apart, in order that the "merlon" or parapet between them should not be too weak. Mantlets or shutters of wood or iron, fascines, &c., are sometimes made to close the neck, (which is only 2 feet wide), as a protection from musketry fire. For field guns the sill should be $3\frac{1}{2}$

feet above the ground. The sole is usually made sloping to the front, unless an elevated fire is required, when it may be countersloping.

The defects of embrasures are that they weaken the parapet, limit the lateral range, act as funnels for the enemy's projectiles, and expose the interior of the work.

Barbettes.—" Gun-banks " are raised platforms of earth, for guns to fire " en barbette " over the crest of the parapet; they are usually made at salient angles, which are filled up, so as to form a short face or "pan coupé," at least 6 feet long. For one gun a gun-bank should be 15 feet wide and 20 feet long. For field guns the gun-bank should be $3\frac{1}{2}$ feet below the crest. A ramp or inclined road is necessary for guns to and from the gun-bank. Barbettes moving have none of the defects of embrasures, their defect is that the guns and gunners are more exposed; to remedy which, "bonnettes" of earth or sand-bags are built up on the superior slope between the guns.

LECTURE XI.

DEFENCE AND ATTACK OF HOUSES.

Defence of Houses.—Houses and small groups of houses, such as farmsteads, often form valuable tactical points on a battlefield, as for example "Hougomont," on the field of Waterloo. Strongly built and well-fortified houses form good reduits in a village, or wood; and are also of value as isolated posts on the line of communications of an army, as at " Rorke's Drift."

Houses, however, cannot be considered defensible against artillery; they may be taken by surprise, especially at night, set on fire, or attacked openly by day.

A house may be put in a fairly good state of defence in about three hours; as a rough guide to the garrison required, allow two men to each door, window, or loophole to be defended, and a reserve of one-fourth.

To guard against surprise and attempts to set the house on fire, a few scouts should be sent out when a siege is expected.

The following is the method of putting a house, or small group of houses, in a state of defence:—

Remove the thatch and other combustibles, and provide water, barricade and loophole the doors and windows, loophole the walls, and clear away all cover round the house.

Then, if not pressed for time, improve the interior communications, make arrangements to defend one room after another, secure ventilation and light, make tambours and machicoulis galleries for flank defence, make and arrange obstacles, loophole and place in a state of defence the garden walls, fences, outhouses, &c., and dig shelter trenches to connect the outer defences, which should be well in advance of the house, as a first line of defence; taking care that the retreat to the house is secure.

The above are the principal points to be attended to; there are many others which vary with every situation and which experience and intelligence will suggest; as a general rule select and improve whatever is useful, and destroy whatever is hurtful.

Attack on a House.—Houses may be attacked and taken by surprise, especially at night; but an open attack by day would be made as follows:—

If guns or rockets are available, the house will soon be destroyed, but if not the house must be attacked on different sides at the same time. The salient angles are the best points of attack, and the advance should be made over ground least exposed to fire.

First of all, the skirmishers advance and keep up a brisk fire, principally at the loopholes, keeping well under cover; these are followed by the storming party accompanied by the engineers, who advance rapidly with bags of powder, crowbars, ladders, beams of wood, &c., to blow open or burst open the doors, windows, walls, &c., and set the house on fire.

HASTY DEMOLITIONS.

Hasty Demolitions.—Gunpowder and guncotton are used for hasty demolitions; the latter is more suitable, being more portable and from two to three times as powerful, and from not requiring so much tamping. Dynamite is sometimes used; it is very nearly as strong as guncotton, it is made up into cartridges and fired by means of a detonator.

Guncotton is made in discs and slabs and will explode whether wet or dry, by means of a detonator containing fulminate of mercury and a primer of dry guncotton.

Powder is sometimes ignited by electricity, but usually by means of a fuze; Bickford's fuze, which burns at the rate of 3 feet per minute, is generally used. Bickford's instantaneous fuze is waterproof and burns at the rate of 30 yards per second.

Bridges, Barricades, Doors, &c.—To destroy an average masonry bridge, a charge of 500 lbs. powder should be placed in a trench 18 inches deep over the keystone of an arch. Two charges placed in trenches over the haunches will produce more effect, but will take longer; the powder is ignited by Bickford's fuze.

A stockade, or barricaded door, or gate may be destroyed by hanging 50 lbs. guncotton from a nail, gimlet, or pickaxe, against the lock, bolt, or hinges, or by placing 60 lbs. powder in tarred sand-bags, well tamped or covered over with sand-bags, against it on the ground, and igniting by means of Bickford's fuze.

Railways, Telegraphs, &c.—To destroy a railway, remove or destroy a few rails, sleepers, and chairs, remove the rolling stock, blow up the bridges, blow in the tunnels, and obstruct the cuttings, and make gaps in the embankments.

A locomotive may be disabled by screwing down the safety valves, firing a shot through the boiler, or firing a charge of powder inside it.

A line of telegraph may be destroyed by cutting down some of the posts and cutting the wires.

LECTURE XII.

DEFENCE AND ATTACK OF VILLAGES, POSITIONS, WOODS, AND BRIDGES.

Villages.—Villages, if not exposed to artillery fire, are capable of a strong defence, and often form valuable tactical points on a battle-field. The village of St. Privat at the battle of Gravelotte, on the French right, was the strongest point of their position; it was not much exposed to fire, and though carried eventually, chiefly through failure of ammunition, it made a brave and obstinate resistance for nearly twelve hours; its capture made the French position untenable and decided the battle.

The defence of a village may be divided into three stages, namely, the exterior line, the village itself, and the reduit or citadel.

The exterior line is far the most important stage;

a line is taken up outside the village, and at least 40 yards from it (so as to be clear of the houses), formed by the hedges, banks, walls, &c., connected where necessary by shelter trenches; all cover in front of this line should be destroyed, and as much flank defence as possible provided by means of small earthworks, such as redans, and by taking advantage of the re-entering angles. Natural obstacles should be improved, and artificial ones made. The walls and hedges running parallel to the front should be levelled, so that they may not afford cover to the enemy during his advance. This exterior line is defended by the fighting line, in rear of which, under cover and near at hand, are the supports; the reserve will be either in the village itself or in rear of it. The artillery is usually posted on the flanks and a little retired, so as to command the approaches, and is seldom placed within the defensive line.

Every effort must be made to hold the exterior line, but if it is lost, the village itself, which should at first have been as strongly fortified as time and means permitted, more especially at the salients, must be held step by step, the streets being barricaded and enfiladed by Gatling guns; and if the village is to be held till the very last, the citadel or strongest building in the village should be defended.

Attack of Village.—As the attackers usually suffer very heavy loss, it would often be better to turn than to attack a well-defended village. But if an attack is decided upon, it should be preceded by a heavy artillery fire. The Germans concentrated two hundred guns against St. Privat, but it was an uphill fire, and did not produce great results, as the village from the nature of the ground was not much exposed. After the artillery has produced sufficient effect, the infantry advances in the attack formation. This attack should be made on salients, and on several points at the same time, so as to distract the attention of the defenders.

Positions.—Positions may be strengthened in a few hours, previous to a battle, by hasty fortification. It rarely happens that more than a few hours are available, so that inclosed earthworks, which come under the head of deliberate fortification, could not be made. But shelter-trenches and gun-pits and gun epaulments, and a few open works such as redans at important points, should first be thrown up, and improved afterwards if time and means permitted. Before tracing shelter-trenches, the slope of the hill should be carefully studied, and the tracing should be such as to permit of the greatest amount of frontal and flanking fire within range of the defenders' weapons. It is not always necessary to have one long continuous line of shelter trench, and openings should always be left for cavalry and artillery to pass through if necessary. The top of the steepest part of the slope will generally mark the line for the shelter trench, but it is more important to clearly see the enemy during the whole of his advance, than to conceal the defenders from fire. A steep slope is therefore much more difficult to defend than a gentle one, because the defenders are obliged to expose themselves in order to fire down it.

Woods.—A wood, before being occupied for defence, should be carefully examined as to its length, depth, thickness, clearings, roads, streams, hills, marshes, houses, &c. It may be artificially strengthened by constructing obstacles at the entrance, and by making inner lines of defence.

The salients of a wood, being most vulnerable, may be strengthened with abatis and entanglements, and the roads by which the enemy will advance may be either broken up or obstructed.

The defenders of a wood have the advantage of cover, whilst the attackers are much exposed. Some woods are thin enough to be passable by all arms; others so thick that infantry only can traverse them when extended.

There are three stages of defence, namely, the exterior or front line, the interior, and the rear line.

The exterior line is by far the most important stage, and every effort must be made to hold it. If there are no banks or ditches, shelter trenches should be thrown up just inside the edge, and if time permit, all cover in front should be destroyed and obstacles arranged in front of the salients. The fighting line will occupy the edge of the wood, the supports being from 50 to 100 yards behind it, and the main body in rear of all in a central position. As the salients will most probably be attacked, they should be strongly guarded, and as much flanking fire as possible provided for them from the re-entering angles. The artillery, as in the case of villages, bridges, fords, &c., should be posted so as to command, or enfilade the approaches, and should be on or near a road, so as to be able to advance and retreat; it should not be inside the wood if there are suitable positions on the flanks.

If the defenders are driven from the front line they can then dispute the interior of the wood, step by step, retreating slowly, until they come to a position capable of defence, such as a fence, bank, or intrenchment, with a clearing in front or the crest of a hill.

Tactical formations, however, cannot be maintained inside a wood, and the fighting will be in groups under section leaders. Supervision in a wood is difficult and men are very apt to get out of hand. The attackers are now on an equality with the defenders, and the fighting on both sides is carried on by the infantry only.

If the defenders are driven through the wood, they can still take up a position on the other side. They should retire from the edge, however, and place their troops in a position strengthened by shelter trenches and gun-pits, commanding all the roads and paths leading out of the wood. Abatis and entanglements may be placed across the roads and paths, at the edge of the wood, and also at the salients.

Attack of Wood.—The attackers have the disadvantage of being seen by, and of not being able to clearly see the defenders. The attack is commenced as usual by artillery fire, on whatever can be seen of the defenders, more especially on their artillery, as soon as its position is disclosed. After this has produced its effect, the infantry advances against the wood in the attack formation; every effort must be made to carry the edge of the wood, because when once inside the attackers are on an equality with the defenders, and will begin to push them back gradually through the wood. The fighting now on both sides will be carried on by the infantry in groups. The attacking infantry will have to be reformed before issuing from the wood. The attacking artillery and cavalry cannot of course act in the wood itself, but will either move round the flanks or follow the infantry through the wood, if there are suitable roads or paths.

Bridges.—The best position for the defence of a bridge is usually in rear of it, but if suitable cover exists or can be made, part of the defending force may sometimes be pushed forward beyond the bridge.

The position taken up should be as close to the bridge as the nature of the ground permits, the infantry should be in shelter-trenches, the artillery in gun-pits, all the approaches to the bridge on the enemy's side should be commanded and enfiladed by artillery and infantry fire, and fire should be concentrated on the bridge itself, the passage of which may be made more difficult by abatis and barricades.

The attackers must first by artillery and infantry fire subdue the fire of the defence before they can advance to force the passage of the bridge.

TACTICS.

LECTURE I.

THE GENERAL FUNCTIONS OF THE THREE ARMS.

STRATEGY is the science of directing great military movements; the Duke of Wellington, Napoleon I., and Count von Moltke are examples of celebrated strategists.

Tactics is the art of manœuvring a military force previous to and during the course of an action, there are therefore tactics of manœuvre and fighting tactics.

Infantry.—Infantry is the most important of the three arms, and battles are almost invariably lost or won by it. Sometimes artillery or cavalry may for a time act the most important part, but on the whole the action of both must be considered as auxiliary to that of infantry.

Its characteristics are mobility and fire action; it can move freely where cavalry and artillery cannot move at all, and its weapons are equally effective for attack and defence; its weapons are the rifle and bayonet.

A battalion of infantry consists of eight companies

of 100 men each; a brigade consists of three battalions; a division consists of two brigades of infantry, a battalion of rifles, a regiment of cavalry, three batteries field artillery, and one company of engineers.

An army corps consists of three such divisions, together with the corps artillery and engineers and a brigade of cavalry. An army consists of several army corps.

Cavalry.—The power of cavalry lies in the offensive, it has little defensive power, and should never therefore receive an attack halted. It requires long training and is expensive to equip. It manœuvres in column and fights in line, but can only act on suitable ground. Its characteristics are speed and shock, its weapons carbines, lances, swords, and pistols. It marches in fours, sections, or half-sections—that is to say, eight, four, or two horses abreast—but it usually marches in sections along a road. The tactical unit is the squadron; a regiment of cavalry consists of four squadrons of 120 men and horses each; a brigade consists of three regiments and one battery of horse artillery.

Artillery.—The great value of artillery consists in its immense range, great accuracy, and its heavy and destructive projectiles. As a rule, infantry and cavalry are held back in action until the artillery has produced an impression on the enemy. Its characteristic is long range fire action. It occupies great space on the march, requires large supplies, is very liable to casualties, is powerless whilst in movement, and can only act on suitable ground.

Field batteries are armed with 9, 13, and 16 pounders; horse artillery with 9 and 13 pounders; mountain artillery with 7 pounders; all of which fire three kinds of projectiles, namely, common shell, shrapnel shell, and case shot. The tactical unit of artillery is the battery, which consists of six guns and six waggons.

Security and Information.—The success of military operations depends a great deal upon good information concerning the country and the enemy, also upon good marching, and a well-organised system of supply and transport, and upon taking the necessary precautions against surprise both when halted and when on the march.

To obtain early, ample, and accurate information about the country, as well as concerning the position, strength, and movements of the enemy, is the first and great object of every general, and is really the first step to victory. This information is gained by selected officers, by scouts, and by reconnoitring parties of cavalry, also by spies, and by questioning prisoners, deserters, and the inhabitants of the country.

Good information is essential to security. On the march, security is obtained by the screening of reconnoitring cavalry, by advanced and rear-guards, and if necessary by flanking parties. Security when halted or encamped is obtained by outposts and by patrols.

LECTURE II.

SPACE AND TIME REQUIRED FOR TROOPS.

A KNOWLEDGE of the space occupied by troops in various formations, and of the time required for troops to move from one place to another, is very necessary for all those who have to issue or to carry out orders for parades and movements.

Infantry.—In line each man occupies 2 feet of front; therefore as there are two ranks a battalion of 800 men will occupy 800 feet of front. If there were eight companies in this battalion you must add 24 feet for twelve officers and colours. Therefore the battalion would require 824 feet or 275 yards, either when drawn up in line or when marching along a road in fours. Between companies in column there is wheeling distance, in quarter column 5 yards. Between battalions in line or on the march the interval is 25 yards. In a line of quarter columns the interval between battalions is 25 yards unless otherwise ordered. The rate of marching is 120 paces or 100 yards a minute, but for long distances including halts, 3 miles an hour.

Infantry marches in fours and fights in extended order (4 paces from file to file).

Cavalry.—Each horse requires 1 yard of front, therefore as there are two ranks a squadron of 120 horses or 60 files would require 60 yards.

There is a distance of a horse's length, namely 8 feet, between the front and rear ranks; the squadron and troop leaders are a horse's length in front of the front rank, and the serrefile rank is a horse's length in rear of the rear rank. A squadron is therefore $7 \times 8 = 56$ feet or 19 yards in depth.

The interval between squadrons in line is 12 yards, and between regiments in line 24 yards. In marching in fours the length of the column in yards is equal to the number of files plus the squadron intervals. In sections it is double the number of files. In half-sections it is four times the number of files.

A regiment of cavalry consisting of four squadrons of sixty files each would, therefore, when drawn up in line, occupy a front of 276 yards. If marching in fours it would occupy 276 yards of road. If marching in sections it would occupy 480 yards, and if in half-sections 960 yards.

Cavalry walk 4 and trot $8\frac{1}{2}$ miles an hour, but for long distances, trotting and walking alternately, 5 miles an hour.

Artillery.—When a battery is in action the six guns are drawn up in line at intervals of 19 yards; the front of the battery is therefore 95 yards. The six waggons are drawn up in rear out of fire.

SPACE AND TIME REQUIRED FOR TROOPS.

The intervals between batteries in line are 28½ yards. The interval between artillery and either of the other arms is also 28½ yards. Two batteries in line therefore have a front of 218½ yards.

On the march a battery moves in column of route, each gun being followed by its own waggon. Each gun or waggon with its six horses is 15 yards long, and the intervals between guns and waggons are 4 yards. A battery will therefore require $12 \times 15 + 11 \times 4$ yards $= 224$ yards of road. Field batteries walk as a rule, and sometimes trot, and can gallop when necessary; their rate of marching is 4 miles an hour. Horse artillery manœuvres with cavalry and their rate of marching is about the same.

Example of space and time calculation.—In making calculations of space for the three arms combined, it is most convenient to calculate for each arm separately, and then to add the intervals between the arms.

As an example, calculate the front of the following force drawn up in line: Two squadrons cavalry of 60 files each; two battalions of infantry 800 men each (in eight companies); and two batteries of field artillery.

	Yards.
Cavalry = $60 \times 2 + 12$ yards	= 132
Infantry = $824 \times 2 + 75$ feet = 1723 feet	= 574
Artillery = $95 \times 2 + 28\tfrac{1}{2}$ yards	= 218½
Interval between Cavalry and Infantry	= 25
Interval between Infantry and Artillery	= 28½
Total	978 yards.

To calculate the length of the above force on the march; the cavalry in sections, infantry in fours, and the artillery in column of route:—

	Yards.
Cavalry = 60 × 2 × 2 yards	= 240
Infantry is the same as in line	= 574
Artillery = 224 × 2 + 28½ yards	= 476½
Interval between Cavalry and Infantry	= 25
Interval between Infantry and Artillery	= 28½
Total	1344 yards.

If a combined force of cavalry, infantry, and artillery were marching together, it is evident that their rate of marching must be that of the slowest marchers, namely, the infantry; so that the time taken by the above force to pass a certain house on the road would be $\frac{1344}{100} = 13\frac{1}{2}$ minutes.

LECTURE III.

ADVANCED GUARDS.

ADVANCED guards are necessary to conceal and cover the movements of the main body, to gain intelligence of the enemy, and to prevent the main body from being attacked or interrupted during the march, or from coming too suddenly into collision with the enemy.

They may be composed of infantry only, or of

cavalry only, but are usually composed of all arms so as to have tactical independence. Their strength should be in proportion to that of the whole force, and should be sufficient to hold their own for a time, until reinforced by the main body. For a division this is usually about one-fourth, but for a smaller force less.

As a rule, the duty of the advanced guard at the end of a march is to form the outposts, and when the camp or bivouac is completed it is relieved.

Infantry Advanced Guard. — The leading company of an infantry advanced guard would be divided into two half-companies; the leading half-company would be under the command of a subaltern, and would detach two files 100 yards to the front, two files 100 yards to the right front, and two files 100 yards to the left front. The other half-company under the captain would follow in support 200 yards in rear, and would detach a connecting file 100 yards to the front, and drop a connecting file 100 yards in rear. The main body would follow 300 yards behind the rear half-company, and would detach a connecting file 100 yards to the front.

Cavalry Advanced Guard.—The principle of the formation of a cavalry advanced guard is the same as that of any other advanced guard, namely, that it should consist of a number of bodies increasing in strength, from front to rear. If a squadron were to form an advanced guard, a non-commissioned officer and about eight or ten men in groups of two in extended order would form the advanced party, followed at an interval of about 500 yards by a support of half a troop under an officer, followed at an interval of about 400 yards by the rest of the squadron, namely, one and a-half troops under the squadron leader.

Small Advanced Guard of All Arms.—A small advanced guard consisting of one battalion, one squadron, two guns, and a party of engineers, would have its squadron of cavalry in front, thrown out much in the same way as above; the battalion would come next, followed by the two guns and the engineers.

Large Advanced Guard of All Arms.—A large advanced guard, consisting of three battalions, four squadrons, one battery and a party of engineers, would be divided in a "van-guard," and the main body of the advanced guard.

The van-guard would consist of one squadron, one battalion, and the party of engineers.

The squadron would lead much in the same order as above, and would be followed by the battalion and the engineers, who would if necessary repair roads and bridges and remove obstacles, &c. The rest of the advanced guard would form the main body of the advanced guard, and at an interval of about 600 yards would follow in support in the following order: one battalion, one battery, one battalion, three squadrons. The chief duty of the van-guard would be to reconnoitre and prepare the way; that of the main body of the advanced guard to support the van-guard and fight. Guns as a rule would not accompany the van-guard; and the cavalry, not required to reconnoitre, would be in rear of the main body of the advanced guard.

The commander of the advanced guard would be in constant communication with the general commanding, to whom he should report all information obtained concerning the country and the movements of the enemy. He should endeavour to insure the security of the march, and attack and drive in any small parties of the enemy. If necessary he should take up a good defensive position, but not attack or bring on a general engagement without orders; and he should carry out the special orders which he receives from the general commanding.

Battle of Nachod, June 1866.—The action of Nachod, in Bohemia, is an example of advanced guard duty well performed. An army corps, of the Crown Prince's army, was traversing the long and narrow defile of Nachod. Its advanced guard, consisting of seven battalions, thirteen squadrons, and three batteries, commanded by Steinmetz, after leaving the defile, found itself opposed by an Austrian force of about three times its strength. Steinmetz, well informed of this by the cavalry of his van-guard, advanced with all his force and took up a strong defensive position in his front, and was there attacked by the Austrians, under General Ramming. For three hours, however, he held his ground, when the Prussian corps, emerging from the defile, reinforced him. The Prussians then took the offensive and advanced against the Austrians, who were eventually compelled to retreat on Skalitz.

LECTURE IV.

REAR-GUARDS.

A REAR-GUARD is an advanced guard reversed, being formed in exactly the same way but turned to the rear.

Rear-guards are necessary to prevent attack or interruption during a march, delay a pursuing enemy, and protect the rear of the column during advance and retreat; they may be composed of infantry only, or of cavalry only, but are usually composed of all arms so as to have tactical independence. Their strength and composition must depend upon the nature of the country, and the manner of pursuit, &c., but should be proportioned to that of the whole force, and in many cases about one-fifth of it.

The duties of a rear-guard during an advance are simply to guard the rear of the column, and the baggage train from the attacks of robbers, disaffected tribes, &c., and to prevent straggling; during a retreat, however, they are far more difficult and important, and consist in constantly making head against a pursuing enemy. A rear-guard then forms a barrier between the pursued and the pursuers, and saves the retreating force from constant attacks and interruptions, and gains time for it to withdraw out of danger and reorganise if necessary. When a force is retreating, after suffering a severe defeat, it incurs the risk of being either captured or cut to pieces. Everything will then depend upon the rear-guard and the skill of its commander.

Marshal Ney was specially distinguished as a rear-guard commander; falling back slowly he delayed the pursuing enemy, and frequently saved the French army from the consequences of defeat.

A rear-guard has usually to fight against the enemy's advanced guard; in order to gain time, it should take up a succession of strong positions, too strong to be attacked by the enemy's advanced guard, until the arrival of their main body. Then the enemy has to reconnoitre the position and change his order of march to order of battle. Then the commander of the rear-guard continues his retreat to another carefully chosen position; he must not have stayed too long, or he will have run the risk of being cut off. It requires great skill to know the exact place and time for taking up a position, and for continuing the retreat. The business then of the rear-guard is in many cases to threaten to fight, rather than actually to fight. It fights, however, sometimes, and even makes counter attacks, but if successful it should not pursue.

There will always be hesitation in attacking a rear-guard well posted, as its strength can seldom be ascertained beforehand, and the pursuers will consequently be in doubt whether they have to deal with merely a rear-guard or with the army itself.

If the rear-guard is strong in cavalry and horse artillery the pursuers will have great difficulty in approaching it, as was the case during the Russian retreat on Moscow. But if the pursuers are strong in cavalry and horse artillery the rear-guard will have a most difficult task, as in the French retreat from Moscow. The cavalry will compel it to keep in close order, and then the fire of the horse artillery will be very effective.

The rear-guard should not be too far behind the main body or it might be cut off, neither should it be too near, or it might be pushed back on the main body.

The distance must depend upon the nature of the country and the manner of the pursuit, &c. If a bridge or defile has to be passed by a retreating force, the rear-guard must at all hazards delay the enemy at some distance from it, so as to give the main body time to pass it safely; as at Constantino during Sir John Moore's retreat to Corunna.

The commander of the rear-guard would of course act in accordance with specific orders from the general commanding, and should if necessary detach flanking parties to watch all parallel roads and take advantage of all strong and suitable positions, to delay the enemy.

Battle of Redinha, March 1811.—The battle of Redinha, during the Peninsular war, is a good example of a rear-guard delaying pursuit.

Wellington was closely pursuing Massena, who was falling back from before the lines of Torres Vedras: the French rear-guard was commanded by Ney, who taking up a strong position at Redinha, succeeded in delaying the pursuit for several hours, and finally having secured the retreat of the French army, withdrew in safety.

LECTURE V.

OUTPOSTS.

OUTPOSTS are thrown out for the security of a force, when halted or encamped. Their duties are observation and resistance. Generally speaking they are composed of all arms, either separately or in combination. Cavalry as a rule are more useful for open country and by day, and are thrown much further forward than infantry. The latter are used for close or wooded country, and by night. Artillery might be used in combination either with cavalry or infantry in special cases, such as guarding a bridge or defile, &c.

A force when halted or encamped in an enemy's country cannot be considered safe from surprise until the outposts are thrown out.

The outposts should cover the front and overlap the flanks, should not be too far from the camp, or the enemy might penetrate the interval, and not too close or they might suddenly be driven in before they had time to warn the main body of the enemy's approach. Their strength should not be greater than sufficient to afford security: in recent wars it has varied from 200 to 800 per mile, according as the country was open or close.

The outposts are composed of picquets, supports, and reserve; the whole being commanded by a field officer called the "commander of the outposts." The picquets are in the front line, the supports about 800 yards in rear of them, and the reserve about 1600 yards in rear of the supports. A battalion of eight companies would usually have two companies on picquet, two in support, and four in reserve.

Infantry Picquets.—A company of about 50 men would form a good picquet, and should be divided into four sections, namely three reliefs and patrol. The captain receives his information and orders from the commander of the outposts, and marches his picquet to its ground, as an advanced guard on a plain. Under cover of a section extended in front, he posts his chain of double sentries, whose front would be about 800 yards, and about 400 yards in rear of the centre of his chain of sentries he stations the picquet itself.

He should be careful afterwards to visit the post of each sentry, and make any alterations that he may on second thoughts think necessary, and alter the position of the picquet if he thinks fit.

At night a picquet should be on or near a road, and closer to its sentries than by day, and fires should not be lighted without permission. Picquets are relieved at daybreak, and as attacks are usually made at that hour, greater vigilance is then required. A mounted orderly with a picquet to carry information and reports to the rear is often very useful.

Sentries.—Sentries are always posted double, and should have an extensive view to the front and flanks, and not be exposed to view; they should be connected with the sentries on the right and left, and with the picquet. Each sentry should be told where the picquet is, and where the neighbouring sentries, and the examining guard (if there is one) are, and where the enemy is expected to come from. In the case of a wood, sentries should be extended along its further edge and just inside it.

Sentries should communicate all information to the picquet by signal, or otherwise, and should not fire unless satisfied that the enemy is moving to the attack, and that an alarm is necessary; they should as a rule be increased at night, and moved to lower ground so as to have the benefit of the sky-line. Sentries should be instructed how to receive deserters, flags of truce, &c., and if there is an examining guard no person will be allowed to pass the line except at that point. Between the line of double sentries and the picquet, it is usual to have two single intermediate or connecting sentries.

Patrols.—Patrols are of two kinds: namely, visiting patrols, who visit the sentries, more especially at night, to see that they are alert, &c.; and reconnoitring patrols for service in front of the line of sentries; the latter should not as a rule advance much more than half a mile beyond the line of sentries, and should examine thoroughly any ground which cannot be seen by the chain of sentries.

Examining Guard.—If a road intersects the chain of sentries, the picquet would often furnish an "examining guard" consisting of one non-commissioned officer and four men, to examine and question any one wishing to pass.

Officer Commanding Picquet.—The officer commanding the picquet, as soon as he has taken over his post, should consider and make up his mind, what he would do under various circumstances; he is under the orders of the officer commanding the outposts, and is responsible for the safety of his post;

if attacked, he should reinforce his sentries, send off a report to the officer commanding the outposts, and hold his ground as long as possible; if obliged to fall back, he should do so slowly and in good order.

Supports.—Supports are intended to reinforce the picquets if necessary, and should be about 800 yards in rear of them and in constant communication with them by means of patrols. One company as support would be sufficient as a rule for two companies on picquet.

Reserve.—About one-third of the troops forming the outposts will usually be kept as the reserve. Its position should be central and about 1600 yards in rear of the supports.

Cavalry Picquets.—Almost everything that has been said about infantry picquets applies also to cavalry picquets. As a rule they are composed of from 20 to 30 men, their sentries are also double and are called " vedettes."

A cavalry picquet should not occupy any inclosed space or cramped position, and if stationed at a village, its vedettes should be well in front of the village, and the picquet itself behind it; the horses of cavalry and artillery should be kept constantly saddled and harnessed and only one-third unbridled at a time for feeding and watering.

If either a cavalry or infantry picquet was posted at a bridge, it should take up its position so as to keep the river and the bridge between itself and the enemy.

The strength of a picquet is regulated by the number of sentries, patrols, and examining guards which it has to furnish.

If a picquet had to furnish four double sentries, an examining guard, and patrols, it would require—

	N.C.O.	Men.
Four double sentries at three reliefs =	3	24
Two connecting sentries at three reliefs =	0	6
Sentry over arms at three reliefs =	0	3
Examining guard =	1	4
Patrols, about one-fourth of the whole =	3	12
Total	7	49

LECTURE VI.

RECONNAISSANCE OF THE ENEMY.

THE object of a reconnaissance is to obtain full and accurate information of the enemy's position, strength, and movements; it is usually a cavalry duty, but if a country is unsuited to the use of cavalry, such as a thickly wooded, or mountainous rugged district would be, or if there was no cavalry available, it would be necessary to use infantry.

Reconnoitring is of great tactical importance to every general, and is absolutely necessary for the proper combination of his movements. Napoleon owed much of his success to good reconnoitring, and the Germans during the Franco-German war attached great value to it, and were kept fully informed by their cavalry of the French movements. On the other hand, bad reconnoitring had much to do with the loss of the battles of Waterloo and Sedan and many others, in which the defeated generals were ill informed of their enemy's position and movements.

Reconnaissances of the enemy may be divided into two classes, namely, "secret reconnaissances" and "reconnaissances in force."

Secret Reconnaissances. — Secret reconnaissances require courage, intelligence, caution, and coolness. They are made by an officer either alone or accompanied by a small escort, or by patrols of cavalry, or infantry. In either case the endeavour should be to see and learn as much as possible, to avoid being seen, to avoid fighting, and to bring back a full and clear report of what has been heard and seen.

Patrols.—The usual strength of a cavalry patrol is from 5 to 20 men; it should be under the command of an officer who should have a map or sketch of the country, and before starting should carefully inspect his men and horses, and see to their shoeing, &c., and take care that they have rations, and whatever else is necessary.

The patrol, if necessary, should be accompanied by a trustworthy guide, and should be formed with a view to guard against surprise, two or three troopers in advance, supported by a stronger party, a couple of flankers on each side, and a few men as a rear-guard. No village, defile, or wood should be entered, before being carefully reconnoitred by a file in front, and a file on each flank. Fighting should be avoided, but if suddenly opposed by superior numbers the patrol should fall back slowly, but not further than necessary, and only as long as it is pressed by superior numbers, and should watch the movements of the enemy, sending off a report to the squadron leader. If a patrol meets a party of equal strength, it should keep it in check, and force it to retire if possible. If it meets a party inferior in strength, it should drive it back, or try and take it prisoner. Valuable information may often be obtained by questioning the inhabitants, or any deserters or prisoners that may be taken.

Reconnaissances in Force.—If a general intended to attack an enemy's position, it would be necessary for him to know its nature, strength, and the manner in which it was occupied, so that he might arrange his plan of attack. It is hardly probable that a secret reconnaissance would succeed in this case, on account of the enemy's outposts, and it would become necessary to make a reconnaissance in force.

A reconnaissance in force is made by a general officer, who at the head of a considerable force marches openly towards the enemy, drives in his outposts, and ascertains the real nature and strength of his position, with a view to attacking it subsequently; as at Candahar on the day previous to the battle, and as at Alexandria at the commencement of the Egyptian campaign.

Screening and Reconnoitring Duties of Cavalry.

A large body of cavalry such as a brigade or division is employed to screen an army during its march, and to reconnoitre in front of it; its duties are to gain early, accurate, and full information concerning the enemy, and by acting as a screen between its own army and the enemy, to prevent the latter from gaining information.

An army on the march would move in several parallel columns, and as a rule each division complete would march by a separate road. The cavalry division in the case of an army, and the cavalry brigade in the case of an army corps, would precede the whole force, in order to screen its movements, and at the same time would reconnoitre and obtain full information concerning the enemy. When screening and reconnoitring in front of an army the cavalry division should be accompanied by trustworthy guides, and should advance sufficiently far to establish contact with the enemy, but not too far, or the enemy might penetrate the interval. When once contact with the enemy is gained, it should never afterwards be lost.

During the Franco-German war, the German cavalry division, consisting of 10 regiments, sometimes preceded the army by from 15 to 20 miles and covered a front of about 60 miles.

The extent of front, however, depends a good deal upon the nature of the country, and the power of the commander to control the whole operation, and transmit the information obtained to the general commanding the army.

If the cavalry division is weak, it will be liable to be driven back by the enemy's cavalry division.

Fan-shaped Formation.—It should be thrown out in a fan-shaped formation; that is to say, numerous small parties such as scouts and patrols in the front line, supported by the squadrons to which they belong, and one or two whole regiments in rear of all, and in a central position as reserve.

When once the scouts and patrols come in contact with the enemy, they should never afterwards lose the touch, but should keep the closest watch on his movements.

If the scouts are driven in they fall back slowly on the patrols; if the patrols are not strong enough to hold their own, they fall back on the squadrons in support, and the squadrons in their turn, if hard pressed, retire on the reserve.

A good system of communication between all the various parts of the fan should be established, so that information may quickly be transmitted from front to rear.

LECTURE VII.

MARCHES.

The success of military operations depends in a great measure upon good marching.

If the soldier is able to march well, and to use his weapons effectively, is properly provided for by the commissariat officer, and is well led by the military officer, then the commander will be in a position to carry out his plans successfully, and to bring his troops to any required place, at the proper time, in sufficient numbers and in an efficient condition.

As a rule each division complete marches on a separate road; if a larger force such as an army corps marched on one road, the length of the column would be something like 26 miles, the march would be very slow, perhaps only one mile an hour, transport and supply difficult to obtain, and if the enemy were met with, the leading troops would probably be beaten before the column could deploy into order of battle.

On the other hand, if the force was disunited, or if there were too many small columns, the enemy might meet them and beat them in detail.

An army corps would therefore usually march on at least three parallel roads, communication being kept up between the divisions, and it should be able to concentrate when necessary at any required point.

Order of March.—When near the enemy the order

of march should be so arranged that it can quickly be changed to order of battle: some cavalry in front, followed by some infantry; next comes all the artillery, followed by the remainder of the infantry; lastly the remainder of the cavalry, followed by the baggage train, and rear-guard.

When not near the enemy, tactical units should not be divided as a rule, but the precise order of march is of minor importance.

Rate of Marching.—The rate of marching depends mainly upon health, discipline, and weather, the state of the roads, and the traffic on the roads. In brigade the average is—infantry 3 miles an hour, artillery 4 miles an hour, and cavalry and horse artillery 5 miles an hour, trains of waggons 2 miles an hour. In a division it would be rather less.

If there is any choice of roads when not near the enemy, artillery should have the best and hardest, cavalry the smoothest, and infantry the shortest.

Halts.—The fatigues of a march should be lessened by the commander in every possible way; frequent halts during a day's march are necessary, and the commander regulates them according to circumstances. General Crawfurd in his orders to the light division in Spain directed a five minutes' halt in every hour.

For halting-places at the end of a day's march, it would be necessary to select places where there is both water and fuel.

Halts should not as a rule be made in a town or village, on account of the difficulty of supervision, neither should they be made in a defile if it can be avoided, if there is any danger of being attacked.

The position of the commander during a march, as also during an action, should be made generally known to all concerned.

Rations.—As regards the rations to be carried by the soldier himself during a march, they should be of the most portable description, and those least likely to be injured by being knocked about in his mess tin. There is perhaps nothing better than bacon, sausage, rice, biscuit, coffee, "pemmican," and what is well known at the Cape by the name of "billtong."

Flank Marches.—When a force on the march exposes its flank to an enemy's attack, it is said to make a flank march; flank marches are sometimes necessary, but they should not be made within reach of a superior force; flanking parties should be sent out on the exposed flank to screen and reconnoitre, and move parallel to the column.

Night Marches.—Night marches are sometimes necessary, but are not advisable under ordinary circumstances, as they are more fatiguing, very liable to straggling and disorder, and the columns are apt to lose their way. Guides would usually be necessary, and so would landmarks at cross roads, and along the routes; detaching parties should be avoided, and there should be no firing on account of the danger of causing alarm and panic.

Forced Marches.—Forced marches are sometimes absolutely necessary, as in the case of Sir Frederick Roberts' celebrated march from Cabul to Candahar; but unless the troops are of very good quality, a few forced marches would seriously diminish the strength of the column.

LECTURE VIII.

INFANTRY.

THERE have been four recognised systems of infantry tactics, namely, those of Frederick the Great, Napoleon, Wellington, and the present or modern system.

Frederick's system was an attack in two parallel lines in an oblique and outflanking direction; its success was due to the application of superior force at a decisive point. The movement however, though well adapted to that period, was a slow and heavy one, and as manœuvring power increased it lost its value and finally collapsed before Napoleon, who met it in front and attacked it in flank at Austerlitz.

Napoleon's system was an attack in battalion columns at deploying intervals, covered by a thick line of skirmishers. Sometimes these columns deployed into line and opened fire, but reformed column before continuing the advance.

Wellington's system was a defensive one, but he also used the line formation for attack. The army was drawn up in two lines, just behind the crest of a hill, and received the enemy with a volley, followed by a charge, the pursuit being carried on by skirmishers. This system was not, and could not be followed by other Continental powers, as no other troops could fight in a line of two ranks.

Modern System.—The column and line formations however had both to give way, when improved and breech-loading fire-arms were adopted, and since the campaigns of 1866 and 1870, it has been universally allowed that fire action in extended order is alone to be depended on, and that not only can infantry use their arms better in extended order, but that it is the only safe way to attack and defend a position: moving in close order under fire is now impossible.

The modern system was partly discovered by accident during the late wars. The infantry extended without orders, and it was found that they fought much better by doing so, having more freedom in using their rifles, and presenting a more difficult target to the enemy. Fire action was formerly merely preparatory to a charge, but it is now the actual means of deciding a battle.

Attack Formation.—The modern attack formation combines the greatest development of fire with great mobility, and the most difficult target for the enemy. The enemy's resistance is first broken down by fire, and then his position is assaulted by the whole attacking force.

As soon as the artillery has made sufficient impression on the enemy, the infantry advances to attack him. Each battalion extends for attack as soon as it comes under the enemy's artillery fire, and is divided into three portions—the fighting line, supports, and main body. The fighting line keeps up a steady fire on the enemy as soon as it gets within range; the supports follow and supply losses and reinforce when necessary, the main body follows and is eventually brought into the fighting line, bayonets are fixed and the position is assaulted. During the advance every advantage is taken of cover, and the supports and main body are extended when necessary.

When a division acting alone advances to the attack, one brigade in extended order forms the first line, the other brigade about 850 yards in rear of it forms the second line, and the divisional infantry battalion about 1200 yards in rear of the second line forms the reserve.

Defence Formation.—A battalion in the first line of defence, forms for defence much in the same manner as for attack: the fighting line in shelter trenches, or under cover, commanding the ground if possible in front for about 1000 yards; the supports well under cover and near at hand; the main body is at first in a central position, so that after the attack has developed itself, it may be moved wherever it is most required.

As soon as the attacking force arrives within the effective range of musketry, the fighting line should at any threatened point be as thick as is compatible with a free use of the rifle.

LECTURE IX.

CAVALRY.

OWING to the immense range and precision of modern fire-arms, cavalry is not now used in masses as it used to be in and about the time of Napoleon.

Its principal uses now are to precede an army on the march, and screen its movements from the enemy, also to reconnoitre and ascertain the position, strength, and movements of the enemy; it is also of great value when a rapid advance is necessary to accomplish a desired object.

Ground.—The ground best suited to the action of cavalry is an open country with a smooth surface, undulating and slightly wooded; if too open, cavalry cannot effect surprises and will be also exposed to fire. Hidden ravines, brooks, rough ground, and deep ditches have spoilt many cavalry charges, and the best way to avoid those dangers is, if possible, to reconnoitre the ground beforehand by sending out scouts.

Supports and Reserve.—A body of cavalry, unless very small, should be formed in two or three lines, the second and third line forming supports and reserve, because even a successful charge produces disorder, and necessitates the victorious cavalry re-forming. The second and third line protect the first line whilst it re-forms behind them and are available to follow up a success or to cover a retreat.

At the battle of Waterloo, Ponsonby lost half his cavalry brigade, because after a successful charge he had no reserve to meet the charge of the French reserve.

As the weak points of all arms are the flanks, a commander should endeavour to protect his own and take every opportunity of attacking those of his enemy. For this reason the best position for the second line will be in rear of the flanks of the first line; the third line, if there is one, may be either in rear of the centre, or in rear of the most exposed flank. The intervals between the lines are usually about 300 yards.

The Charge.—The charge to be effective should be sudden, rapid, and opportune, and the pace so regulated and gradually increased as to be greatest at the moment of collision; but it must be slow at first, and in a good line. If too fast the horses will be blown and unfit for further efforts after the charge. Many instances of this have occurred after successful but too rapid charges. If the charge is not sudden, the opportunity of effecting a surprise would probably be lost. It should be opportune, because favourable chances occur but seldom, and often quickly pass away for ever. A charge down a slight incline increases the impetus, but unless an incline is very slight, disorder would occur either in charging up or down it.

Cavalry acting against cavalry should seek to take it in flank, or to surprise it whilst manœuvring or whilst engaged with other troops. Cavalry is not now formidable to good infantry, well posted and on its guard, owing to the increased mobility and improved fire-arms of the latter; but it often gets chances during a battle of taking infantry by surprise, and in flank, and when engaged with other troops, and when broken and disordered; and then the action of cavalry is most effective. As a direct attack on artillery would be too costly, cavalry should seek to attack it in flank or in rear, part moving against the covering party and part in extended order against the guns. Artillery surprised, unsupported, or whilst in movement, falls an easy prey to cavalry.

Fighting on foot.—Occasions may occur, and during the Franco-German war they frequently did occur, for cavalry to dismount in order to fight, skirmish, or reconnoitre on foot; the rear rank acting as horse-holders to the front rank. If necessary, a horse-holder can hold three horses as well as his own.

LECTURE X.

ARTILLERY.

FIELD batteries are armed with 16, 13, and 9-pounders; horse artillery with 13 and 9-pounders; and mountain artillery with 7-pounders.

As 3000 yards is about the maximum distance that a man can see sufficiently well to lay a gun, this must consequently be taken as the greatest range, and as infantry fire is effective up to 900 yards, artillery should not, as a rule, come within that distance of the enemy's infantry; but it frequently happens that it is necessary for them to run the risk, expose themselves to infantry fire, and fire case: for instance, in holding a position to the last, arresting a forward movement, following up a victory, or checking a pursuit, or defending themselves from an attack; as the French did at Friedland and Salamanca, and the Prussians at the battle of Wörth.

Position.—The best position is an elevated one with a hard level surface, having an extensive view to the front and flanks, and good lines of advance and retreat; but the slope towards the enemy should be gradual like a glacis; a steep slope produces plunging fire, which is bad.

Cover.—Cover for the guns, gunners, horses, limbers, &c., is a matter of importance, and if the natural cover is not good enough, and time and means permit, some sort of breastwork should be thrown up, such as gun-pits and gun-epaulments.

Change of Position.—As guns are only useful as long as they are stationary and in action, they should not change position as long as their fire continues to be effective, but when this ceases to be the case and they make a forward movement, it should be made rapidly. During the progress of an action it usually becomes necessary for batteries to advance to more forward positions. As a general rule these advances should not be less than 800 yards at a time.

Concentration of Fire.—Concentration of fire is also a matter of importance, and can be obtained in two ways, namely, from batteries "massed" and from batteries "dispersed." Batteries massed offer a very large target to the enemy, and batteries dispersed cannot be controlled by one officer. The nature of the ground sometimes forbids massing and sometimes forbids dispersion. Massing batteries has been found best in practice.

The French massed 100 guns at Wagram; and at Borodino 120 guns at first and afterwards 200. At Wörth the Prussians massed 78 guns against the French centre, and 72 guns against their right.

The great importance of artillery consists in its paving the way for attack ; no infantry attack can be safely made until a heavy artillery fire has made an impression. On the march, therefore, the artillery should be near the head of the column, as it will be first wanted. In attacking a position artillery would first open fire at from 2000 to 3000 yards, but as the infantry gained ground it would move forward to more advanced positions.

Escort.—In exposed positions, in order to protect a battery from skirmishers, and attacks on the flanks and rear, a troop of cavalry or a company of infantry is often attached to it as escort, and is entirely under the direction of the officer commanding the battery. Before advancing to a new position during an action, if there is any chance of danger, a few scouts should be sent forward to reconnoitre; vedettes should also be posted on the exposed flank and rear whilst a battery is in action.

Objective of Artillery.—The ruling principle both in attack and defence is that artillery should fire on whatever is most formidable or most conspicuous at the moment. At the commencement of an action, the attacking artillery should first direct its fire on the defenders' artillery, because until that is more or less subdued, the attacking infantry cannot advance. If, however, the attackers have a great superiority in artillery, part of their guns should fire on the defenders' artillery and part on his infantry.

After the attacking infantry has advanced against the position, the movements and action of the attacking artillery should conform to and support the movements and action of the attacking infantry.

As regards the artillery of the defence, the heaviest guns should occupy the most commanding ground, for the defence of the most important approaches, and should in the first instance open fire on the attacking artillery, and continue the fire until the attacking infantry comes within range, when they should turn the whole of their fire on the attacking infantry. If the attackers have a great superiority of guns at the commencement of a battle, it will sometimes be better for the defensive artillery, instead of engaging in an unequal duel, to withdraw for a time from action, and reserve itself for the approach of the attacking infantry.

LECTURE XI.

THE THREE ARMS COMBINED IN ATTACK.

Artillery.—Every attack should be preceded by a heavy artillery fire from batteries well posted; this fire should be directed on that part of the enemy's force most formidable or most conspicuous at the moment; this would in the first instance usually be the enemy's artillery, because until that is more or less subdued it would be impossible for the infantry to advance. When the artillery has made a sufficient impression, the infantry, which in the meantime has been kept under cover, advances to the attack; from this moment, and for the rest of the day, the movements and action of the artillery and cavalry should be made to conform to and support the movements of the infantry.

Infantry.—At the proper moment the infantry advances against the position in the attack formation: whilst it is doing so the artillery must continue to endeavour to silence the enemy's guns, and break down the resistance of his infantry. As the infantry gains ground, the artillery dashes forward to more advanced positions: should the infantry receive a check, the artillery must try to overcome the cause of the check; should the enemy make a counter attack, the artillery must at once oppose it; and should the infantry succeed in carrying the position, the artillery should advance at once to secure possession of it.

Cavalry.—In the meantime the cavalry takes no active part in the attack; it has ceased to be used in masses, on account of the great range and precision of modern fire-arms. Its duty now during an attack is to keep out of fire, hover about the weakest points, such as the flanks, protect the other two arms from an attack by the enemy's cavalry, and watch for favourable opportunities of taking any portion of the enemy's forces at a disadvantage.

Pursuit and Retreat.—If the attack has been successful and the enemy repulsed and retreating, the cavalry and horse artillery assume a leading part, and follow up the pursuit and are supported by the infantry. If, on the other hand, the attack has failed, they cover the retreat and check the pursuit of the enemy's cavalry.

Principles of Attack.—All attacks should be made with superior force, at decisive points, at the right time. If the opposing forces are nearly equal in numbers, superiority at one point would entail inferiority at another; so that it is necessary whilst applying superior force at decisive points, to so manœuvre the remainder, as to make the enemy believe himself seriously threatened at other points. When the decisive point has been carried by the superior force, the manœuvring force, which has meanwhile been rather held back, advances in concert with the other columns, and the issue of the battle is decided.

The attacker has the following advantages over his opponent: He can choose his own point or points of attack, which would usually be the weakest, or the most important points. He can make false as well as real attacks, and thus keep his enemy uncertain as to his real intentions and force him to conform to his movements.

Modern Tactics.—The defence has gained so much by recent improvements in fire-arms, that a front attack is now rarely practicable, and success can best be obtained by attacking the weakest points; these are in most cases the flanks. A vigorous demonstration should, however, be made against the front, whilst the weight of the attack is pressed against a flank; when the attackers have a great superiority in numbers, both flanks may be attacked, and this is what is called the Prussian or enveloping system, so successful at Wörth.

Ammunition.—Modern fire-arms and the present system of tactics entail the expenditure of enormous quantities of ammunition. It is a matter of great importance that not only sufficient ammunition should be on the ground, but that there should be no delay or difficulty in supplying it to those engaged.

LECTURE XII.

THE THREE ARMS COMBINED IN DEFENCE.

In taking up a defensive position there would usually be a first and second line of defence, and sometimes a reserve. There should be a fixed intention of assuming the offensive as soon as the opportunity occurs; for which purpose a sufficient portion of the force should be kept back out of the fighting line for counter attack.

Infantry.—In defence as well as attack, the result will depend chiefly on the effect of the infantry fire. It is stated that during the Franco-German war from 90 to 92 per cent. of those put "hors de combat" were either killed or wounded by infantry fire. In the same war the French infantry defensive fire was described as effective at 1000 yards. At the defence of Plevna, the Turkish fire was described by Todleben as effective at twice that distance. Such long range fire, however, is only effective against a large body of troops in close order.

Formerly battles were decided by "shock," and after the attackers reached the position. They are now decided by fire, and if the attackers once succeed in reaching their opponents, the latter will not have much chance of success. It is therefore necessary for the defenders to overwhelm the attackers with fire long before they approach close enough to fix bayonets and assault the position. They must therefore open up a well-regulated fire at the greatest range at which it can be made effective.

Artillery.—The best artillery positions having been carefully chosen, the heavy batteries are massed on the most commanding ground, and for the defence of the most important approaches. The ranges should be at once ascertained, so that an effective fire may be opened as soon as the enemy come within 3000 yards. Battles are now usually commenced by an artillery duel, in order that the way may be prepared for the action of the other two arms.

Cavalry.—The cavalry takes no active part in the defence, and it should not be exposed to fire. Its usual place is in rear of the flanks, but it has no fixed place, and is stationed wherever it is thought most likely that it will be required. It protects the other two arms from the attack of the enemy's cavalry, watches for opportunities favourable to its action, and at the end of the battle either follows up the pursuit or covers the retreat.

Principles of Defence.—In the defence of a position, it is not necessary that the troops should be formed in one continued line. Certain important points should be strongly occupied, and others not at all or only very slightly. Flank attacks have to be specially guarded against, and the second line of defence will be available to oppose them. False as well as real attacks are pretty certain to be made; the false attacks cannot be neglected, or they will probably be turned into real attacks; but the real attacks must be opposed by superior numbers. The defender has the following advantages over his opponent. He can select his own position and organise a well-considered plan of defence. Lines of intrenchment will enable him to meet the attack of greatly superior numbers; and the fire of the defenders, who are stationary and well covered, should be far more effective than that of the attackers, who are moving and exposed to fire.

The Commander of a Mixed Force.

The duties and responsibilities of the commander of a mixed force are very great, and require constant thought and care. The most important qualities for a commander are moral and physical courage, coolness, knowledge, and experience in warfare. As he alone is responsible for the failure or success of his operations, he should be guided by his experience and his own judgment; and his constant thought and care should be to gain information of his enemy, and of the country he is operating in; to keep his troops in efficient condition and secure from surprise, both when on the march and when in camp; and to bring them to the right place, at the right time, in sufficient numbers. He should always have a distinct end in view, and make every movement in conformity with it.

MILITARY LAW.

LECTURE I.

THE ARMY ACT—CRIMES AND PUNISHMENTS.

MILITARY LAW is the law by which the Army is governed; its foundation is the Army Act 1881, which is an "Act of Parliament" renewed annually by a short Act of about four pages, called the "Annual Act."

Sections 69 and 70 of the Army Act give power to the Queen to make Articles of War and Rules of Procedure, but only in accordance with the Army Act itself.

Sections 175 and 176 of the Army Act define clearly the persons subject to military law, and divide them into two classes, namely, officers and soldiers.

1. Officers and soldiers of the Regular forces are always subject to military law.

2. The permanent staff of the Auxiliary forces always.

3. The Indian and Colonial forces always.

4. The Militia officers always, and the Militia non-commissioned officers and men during training or embodiment.

5. The Yeomanry during training, or when exercised with the Regulars or Militia.

6. The Volunteers when exercised with the Regulars or Militia.

7. The Reserve forces when called out for training, or in aid of the civil power, or on permanent service.

8. The Royal Marines when serving on shore with the Regular forces.

9. Civilians when permitted to accompany a force on active service.

The Rules of Procedure, the Queen's Regulations, the War Office Army Circulars, General Orders, and Royal Warrants also form part of military law.

Sec. 2.—The Army Act is to remain in force for the period specified in the Annual Act (12 months).

Sec. 3.—The Army Act is divided into five parts: Part I. Discipline. Part II. Enlistment. Part III. Billets and Impressment of Carriages. Part IV. General Provisions. Part V. Application of Military Law, Saving Provisions and Definitions.

CRIMES AND PUNISHMENTS.

Section 4 contains a group of seven offences on *active service* punishable with *death*.

Section 5 contains a group of six offences on *active service* punishable with *penal servitude*.

Section 6 contains a group of eleven offences punishable with *death on active service*, and *imprison-*

ment if not on active service. It also contains a group of two offences punishable with imprisonment only, there being no intention to commit the first offence, and the second offence not having been committed treacherously.

Mutiny and Insubordination.

Sec. 7.—*Mutiny and sedition* is punishable with *death*.

Sec. 8.—1. Striking, using or offering violence to superior in *execution of his office*, is punishable with *death*.

2. The same offence to superior not in the execution of his office, but on *active service*, is punishable with *penal servitude*.

3. The same offence to superior *not* in execution of his office and *not* on active service, is punishable with *imprisonment*.

Sec. 9.—1. Disobedience and *wilful defiance* to superior in *execution of his office* is punishable with *death*.

2. Disobedience to superior on *active service* is punishable with *penal servitude*.

3. Disobedience to superior *not* in execution of his office, and *not* on active service, is punishable with *imprisonment*.

Sec. 10. — Minor cases of insubordination are punishable with imprisonment.

Sec. 11.—Neglect to obey garrison or other orders is punishable with imprisonment.

Desertion.

Sec. 12.—Desertion on *active service*, or under orders for active service, is punishable with *death*.

Desertion under other circumstances, for the first offence, imprisonment; for subsequent offences, penal servitude (a previous case of fraudulent enlistment is to reckon as a previous case of desertion).

Sec. 13.—*Fraudulent enlistment* from the Regulars or embodied Militia into Regulars, or from the Regulars into the Militia, the Reserve forces, or the Navy, for the first offence, imprisonment; for subsequent offences, penal servitude (a previous case of desertion is to reckon as a previous case of fraudulent enlistment).

Sec. 14.—Assisting or conniving at desertion is punishable with imprisonment.

Sec. 15.—Absence without leave is punishable with imprisonment.

Disgraceful Conduct.

Sec. 16.—Scandalous behaviour of an officer. For this offence the punishment is peremptory, and the officer *must be cashiered*. For other offences in the Army Act, the officer is *liable to be cashiered*, or to suffer such less punishment as in the Act mentioned.

Sec. 17.—Stealing, misapplying, or embezzling public money *in his charge* is punishable with *penal servitude*.

Sec. 18.—Malingering, maiming, or delaying cure,

stealing from a comrade, or stealing public money, committing any fraudulent act, or disgraceful conduct of a cruel, indecent, or unnatural kind, is punishable with *imprisonment*.

Drunkenness.

Sec. 19.—Drunkenness on duty or not on duty is punishable with imprisonment and a fine not exceeding 1*l*.

Prisoners.

Sec. 20.—Releasing without authority, or allowing a prisoner to escape, *if wilfully, penal servitude; if negligently, imprisonment*.

Sec. 21.—Irregular imprisonment is punishable with imprisonment.

Sec. 22.—Escape from imprisonment is punishable with imprisonment.

Property.

Sec. 23.—Corrupt dealings in supplies is punishable with imprisonment.

Sec. 24.—Deficiency in or injury to kit and equipment is punishable with imprisonment.

False Documents and Statements.

Sec. 25. — False documents and declarations, punishable with imprisonment.

Sec. 26.—Neglect to report and signing in blank is punishable with imprisonment.

Sec. 27.—False accusations and statements, punishable with imprisonment.

Courts-Martial.

Sec. 28.—A military witness not attending, or refusing to be sworn or to produce a document or answer a question, or guilty of contempt of court, is punishable with imprisonment. And a witness, bystander, or the prisoner can, for gross contempt of court, be sentenced summarily and without trial to twenty-one days' imprisonment, by order of the President.

Sec. 29. — False evidence is punishable with imprisonment.

Billeting.

Secs. 30 and 31.—Offences relating to billeting and to impressment of carriages are punishable with imprisonment.

Enlistment.

Sec. 32.—A man discharged with *disgrace* from any part of Her Majesty's forces, or from the Navy enlisting into the Regulars, is punishable with *penal servitude.*

Sec. 33.—False statements or answers on attestation are punishable with imprisonment.

Sec. 34.—Wilfully contravening the enlistment regulations is punishable with imprisonment.

Miscellaneous Offences.

Sec. 35.—Traitorous or disloyal words regarding the Sovereign, punishable with imprisonment.

Sec. 36.—Injurious disclosures, punishable with imprisonment.

Sec. 37.—Striking a soldier or detaining his pay, punishable with cashiering for an officer, and imprisonment for a non-commissioned officer.

Sec. 38.—Duelling, or attempting to commit suicide, is punishable with imprisonment.

Sec. 39.—Refusal to deliver up to the civil power an officer or soldier charged with a civil offence is punishable with imprisonment.

Sec. 40.—Conduct to the prejudice of good order and military discipline is punishable with imprisonment.

Civil Offences triable by Court-Martial.

Sec. 41.—Treason and murder, punishable with *death*; manslaughter, treason-felony, and rape punishable with *penal servitude*. Other civil offences can be punished either as the law of England directs or as offences to the prejudice of good order and military discipline. Provided that offences of treason, murder, manslaughter, treason-felony, and rape, committed in the United Kingdom, cannot be tried by court-martial, neither can they be elsewhere unless committed on active service, or unless the place, not being in the United Kingdom or Gibraltar, is more than 100 miles in a straight line from a competent civil court.

Trafficking in Commissions.

Sec. 155.—The penalty for trafficking in commissions is a fine of 100*l*., or six months' imprisonment. And in the case of an officer convicted by court-martial of this offence, dismissal from the service.

LECTURE II.

THE ARMY ACT—COURTS-MARTIAL.

To avoid frequent repetitions of long words, it has been necessary to abbreviate and substitute C.M. for court-martial, G. for general, D. for district, R. for regimental, F.G. for field-general, S. for summary, C.O. for commanding officer, F.O. for field officer, N.C.O. for non-commissioned officer, and P.S. for penal servitude.

There are five kinds of court-martial, namely, regimental C.M., district C.M., general C.M., field-general C.M., and summary C.M.

Sec. 47.—Regimental C.M. may be convened by officers authorised to convene G.C.M. or D.C.M., or any C.O. not below captain; but on board ship by a C.O. of any rank. The President must be appointed by the convening officer, and not be below captain unless on board ship, the line of march, or when no captain is available. Powers: forty-two days' imprisonment, reduction, fine and stoppages. There must be at least three members, and each must have one year's service.

Sec. 48.—District C.M. may be convened by an officer authorised to convene a G.C.M., or by an officer authorised by him. There must be five members at home, India, Gibraltar, and Malta, and three members elsewhere, and each must have two years' service. The President must be appointed by the convening officer, and be F.O. if possible; but a subaltern if no F.O. or captain is available. Powers: two years' imprisonment, reduction, fine, forfeitures, stoppages, and discharge with ignominy.

General C.M. may be convened by the Queen, or by an officer authorised by the Queen. There must be nine members at home, India, Gibraltar, and Malta, and five members elsewhere, and each must have three years' service. The President must be appointed by the convening officer, and be F.O. if possible, but never below captain; at least five members must be above the rank of subaltern. Powers: death, penal servitude, cashiering, in addition to the powers of a D.C.M. A sentence of death must have the concurrence of two-thirds of the members.

Sec. 49.—Field-general C.M. for the trial of offences against the person or property of inhabitants abroad when an ordinary C.M. is not practicable.

It may be convened by a C.O. of any rank, who may also preside if necessary. There must be not less than three members. Powers: the same as G.C.M., but death must have the concurrence of all the members. No sentence can be executed until confirmed, as provided by Army Act, sec. 54.

Sec. 50.—The members of any C.M. may belong to the same or to different corps, or may be unattached, and may try persons belonging to or attached to any corps. The convening officer shall not sit on any C.M. except F.G.C.M., neither shall the prosecutor, witnesses for the prosecution, the C.O., or the officer who investigated the charge, either sit on a C.M., except F.G.C.M., or act as judge-advocate.

Sec. 51.—Challenges by the prisoner to the President are allowed if supported by one-third of the members; challenges to a member are allowed if supported by one-half of the members.

Sec. 52.—Section 52 contains the oath to members. For the oath to judge-advocate, shorthand writer, interpreter, supernumerary members, and witnesses, *vide* Rules of Procedure 27 and 80.

Sec. 53.—If the President dies or is unable to attend and the court is not reduced thereby below the legal minimum, the senior member may, if of sufficient rank, be appointed President, but if not, the court is dissolved. If the prisoner is too ill to attend before the finding, the court is dissolved.

If the court is dissolved under either of the above circumstances, the prisoner may be tried again.

The court may at any time adjourn, or may be cleared, or may view any place.

If the votes are equal on the finding, the prisoner is acquitted.

If the votes are equal on any other question or the sentence, the President has a second or casting vote.

A recommendation to mercy forms part of the proceedings, and must afterwards be communicated to the prisoner.

Sec. 54.—The following officers have power to confirm findings and sentences:—

R.C.M. The convening officer, or officer having power to convene.

D.C.M. An officer having power to confirm findings and sentences of G.C.M., or an officer authorised by him.

G.C.M. The Queen, or an officer authorised by the Queen.

F.G.C.M. The officer authorised to confirm findings and sentences of G.C.M., of the force of which the detachment forms part.

Revision is only allowable once, and no additional evidence may be received on it. If the finding only is sent back for revision, the court may also revise the sentence.

A sentence cannot be increased on revision.

Acquittal cannot be revised, as it must be pronounced in open court and the prisoner discharged.

If a member of a court-martial becomes confirming officer he cannot confirm that C.M. but must refer it to a superior officer competent to confirm a similar C.M., or to the Governor of a Colony.

A confirming officer may withhold confirmation and refer to superior authority competent to confirm.

Findings and sentences shall not be valid until confirmed, except findings of acquittal.

Sentences of death in a Colony, except for offences on active service, must also be approved by the Governor of the Colony.

Sentences of death in India for treason or murder, except on active service, must also be approved by the Governor-General or Governor of the Presidency.

Sentences of P.S. for manslaughter, rape, or other civil offences must also be approved by the Governor-General, or Governor of the Presidency, or Governor of the Colony, if the trial is within the limits of their authority.

Sec. 55.—On active service, if an ordinary C.M. is not practicable, a summary C.M. may be convened. (Secs. 50 to 54 inclusive are not to apply to it.) If possible there are to be three members, but never less than two. If there are three members its powers are the same as a G.C.M. If only two members its powers are summary punishment or two years' imprisonment. Sentences of death or P.S. cannot be carried out until confirmed by the general or field officer commanding the force.

Sec. 56.—The conviction of a less offence is permissible on the charge of a greater of the same nature. In the cases of stealing and desertion only, the converse of this rule partly holds good.

Sec. 57.—The confirming officer has power to mitigate, remit, commute, or suspend the execution of a sentence. (For remission after confirmation, *vide* Lecture IV.)

Sec. 58.—A sentence of P.S. under Military Law shall have the same effect as if under Civil Law in the United Kingdom.

Sec. 68.—Terms of imprisonment and P.S. are to commence on the day the original sentence was signed by the President; terms of imprisonment, whether under one or more sentences, are not to exceed two consecutive years.

Sec. 122.—A royal warrant is necessary for convening and confirming a G.C.M. Some of these warrants are for convening only, others for convening and confirming, others for convening and confirming and delegating to others the power to convene and confirm G.C.M.

Sec. 123.—Any officer holding a warrant to convene a G.C.M. may convene a D.C.M., or empower any officer not under the rank of captain, under his command, to convene a D.C.M.; and he may confirm a

THE ARMY ACT—COURTS-MARTIAL. 103

D.C.M., and he may also authorise any officer whom he has empowered to convene a D.C.M. to confirm the same.

Sec. 124.—Any person tried by court-martial may, on payment of 2d. per folio of 72 words, have a copy of a G.C.M. within seven years, and of any other C.M. within three years.

Sec. 125.—Any person required as a witness may be summoned in the prescribed manner, and in court, and also in going to and returning from court is privileged from arrest.

Sec. 126.—A civilian witness, if he does not obey the summons to attend, or if he refuses to take the oath, or to produce any necessary document, or to answer a question, or if he is guilty of contempt of court, will, on the President's certificate to that effect, be tried and punished by a court of law; if a civilian witness gives false evidence he may be tried and punished for perjury by a court of law.

Sec. 127.—A court-martial in its proceedings is to be governed by English law only.

Sec. 128.—The rules of evidence are to be the same as those followed in civil courts.

Sec. 129.—Counsel may appear for the prosecution and defence at general courts-martial, and must conform to the rules of courts-martial, and conduct themselves as if before a High Court of Justice. Any offence by counsel may be certified by the President to a court of law.

Sec. 130.—If the court is of opinion that the prisoner is insane and unfit for trial, or that he was insane when he committed the offence, it shall specially find that fact, and the prisoner will be kept in custody pending further instructions. If a prisoner becomes insane during his imprisonment, his removal may be ordered to an asylum, and if he recovers his sanity he may be sent back to prison.

LECTURE III.

THE ARMY ACT—MISCELLANEOUS.

Redress of Wrongs.

Sec. 42.—If an officer thinks himself wronged by his C.O. he may complain to the commander-in-chief.

Sec. 43.—If a soldier thinks himself wronged, he may complain first to his captain, then to his C.O., and then to the general commanding the district.

Punishments.

Section 44 contains the scale of court-martial punishments to which officers and soldiers are liable, and certain provisos.

Summary punishment consists of field imprisonment No. 1. or field imprisonment No. 2. It can only be awarded for certain crimes on active service, namely, crimes punishable with death or P.S.

disgraceful conduct under section 18, and for an aggravated case of drunkenness, which means, drunk on duty, or the line of march, or after being warned for duty, or when too drunk to be warned for duty.

Arrest and Trial.

Section 45 contains the rules as to the arrest, custody, investigation of charges, and trial of officers and soldiers charged with offences.

Powers of C.O.

Sec. 46.—Imprisonment, with or without hard labour, for seven days (168 hours); fine for drunkenness not to exceed 10s.; any authorised deduction from pay (this is not to exceed five days' pay for absence without leave, *vide* Royal Warrant 1882, Article 766).

By the Queen's Regulations, Section VI. paragraph 35, a C.O. may dispose of summarily or try by R.C.M. offences under the following sections of the Army Act, namely, section 10 (except sub-section 1), section 11, section 15 (except absence without leave over twenty-one days), and sections 19, 24, 40.

Drunkenness of a soldier not on duty or not warned for duty *must* be summarily dealt with by C.O. unless it is an aggravated case, or unless there are at least four previous cases in the last twelve months.

Absence without leave from eight to twenty-one days may be punished by as many days' imprisonment as days of absence, the witnesses being examined on oath if the prisoner requires it. A soldier may appeal to a D.C.M. or R.C.M. against imprisonment, fine, or deduction from pay.

Sections 69 and 70 give power to the Queen to make Articles of War and Rules of Procedure in accordance with the provisions of the Army Act.

Sec. 72.—When a soldier has been absent without leave for twenty-one days, a court of inquiry is to assemble and take evidence on oath, and shall declare the illegal absence and the deficiency of clothing, necessaries, &c., if any, and a record of the declarations shall be entered by the C.O. in the regimental books, and be considered legal evidence of the facts.

Sec. 73.—If a soldier signs a confession of desertion or fraudulent enlistment, a competent military authority may dispense with his trial, and may award the same forfeitures and deductions that a court-martial could, or as would be incurred on conviction by court-martial.

A record of confession of desertion, or fraudulent enlistment must always be entered in the regimental books and countersigned by the C.O., and the man is to continue to do duty in the corps, until legal proof can be obtained of his truth or falsehood. The competent military authority, for the purposes of this section, means the commander-in-chief or the adjutant-general, the commander-in-chief of India or of an Indian Presidency, or the officer commanding the troops in a Colony.

Stoppages of Pay.

Sec. 136.—The pay of officers and soldiers shall be subject to no deductions, except those authorised by this or by any other Act or by a royal warrant.

Sec. 137.—The following penal deductions may be made from an officer's pay. 1st. Absence without leave, or overstaying his leave, unless a satisfactory explanation is given. 2nd. Any deduction for loss, damage, &c., awarded by court-martial. 3rd. The sum required to make good the pay of officers and soldiers unlawfully detained by him.

Sec. 138.—The following penal deductions may be made from a soldier's pay. 1st. Desertion, absence without leave, and prisoner of war. 2nd. Imprisonment by civil power, court-martial, or commanding officer. 3rd. Awaiting trial by civil power or court-martial, if afterwards convicted, or under detention for absence if afterwards awarded imprisonment for it by his C.O. 4th. In hospital for sickness caused by an offence under the Army Act. 5th. Any deduction for loss, damage, &c., awarded by court-martial, or commanding officer. 6th. Any stoppage due on account of the Auxiliary forces. 7th. Liquor money on board ship for twenty-eight days. 8th. Fines by civil power, court-martial, or commanding officer. 9th. Maintenance of wife, children, and bastard children.

At least 1$d.$ a day is to be left to the soldier, after making deductions for his messing and washing.

Sec. 139.—Any deduction of pay may be remitted, as provided by royal warrant, or by the Secretary of State.

Sec. 140.—The manner of deducting the pay of officers and soldiers may be regulated by the Secretary of State, and cases of doubt are to be decided by him.

Apprehension of Deserters.

Sec. 154.—Any person suspected of being a deserter, may be apprehended by a constable, or if there is no constable at hand, by an officer or soldier, and brought before a court of summary jurisdiction, and the case will be dealt with as if it were an indictable offence.

Furlough.

Sec. 173.—If a soldier on furlough is detained by sickness, or otherwise, his furlough may be extended for one month, by an officer, not under the rank of captain, performing military duty in the neighbourhood, or by a justice of the peace, but the extension and its cause must be communicated to the soldier's commanding officer, who may, if he thinks fit, cancel the extension.

Indian Forces.

Section 180 contains certain modifications of the Army Act with respect to Her Majesty's forces serving in India.

THE ARMY ACT—MISCELLANEOUS.

1. A court-martial may try any person not subject to military law for an offence as a witness, or for contempt of court-martial.

2. The native army of India is to be governed by Indian military law, enacted by the Government of India.

3. The Governor of a Presidency may suspend the proceedings of a court-martial held on an officer or soldier of Her Majesty's Indian forces.

4. An officer of Her Majesty's Indian forces may complain to the commander-in-chief of the Presidency, who shall submit the case to the Governor of that Presidency.

5. An officer of the Indian staff corps may be sentenced to forfeit part or the whole of his army or staff service.

6. The Governor of a Presidency may reduce a warrant officer, or hospital apprentice, to a lower grade, or to his previous regimental rank.

7. Part II., Enlistment, of the Army Act shall not apply to Her Majesty's Indian forces.

8. An indictable offence means an offence punishable with rigorous imprisonment.

Warrant Officers.

Section 182 contains special provisions as to warrant officers. In addition to the modifications for a non-commissioned officer (sec. 183) they are subject to the following modifications, namely :—

They cannot be punished by C.O., or tried by R.C.M., or sentenced by D.C.M. to any punishment not mentioned in this section.

They may be dismissed, suspended, or reduced to a lower grade, or to the ranks, but not required to serve in the ranks as soldiers. The President of their court-martial must never be below the rank of captain.

Non-Commissioned Officers.

Section 183 contains special provisions as to non-commissioned officers.

(1) The C.O. is not obliged to deal summarily with them for drunkenness. (2) The commander-in-chief at home, India, or Indian Presidency, may reduce them to a lower grade, or to the ranks. (3) A court-martial may reduce them to a lower grade, or to the ranks, with or without other punishment. (4) An army schoolmaster may by court-martial be sentenced to penal servitude, or to imprisonment, or to be reduced to a lower grade, or to be dismissed; or may be dismissed by commander-in-chief at home, India, or Indian Presidency. (5) A commanding officer may reduce an acting N.C.O. to his permanent grade, or if he has no permanent grade, to the ranks.

Persons not belonging to Her Majesty's Forces.

Sec. 184.—Persons not belonging to Her Majesty's forces, but who become subject to military law, may be tried and punished by any C.M. except R.C.M., and the C.O. of such person shall be the C.O. of the corps he is attached to, or the general or officer commanding the force, or any officer named by the officer commanding the force, but such person is not if possible to be placed under command of an officer holding an inferior official rank.

Troops on Board Her Majesty's Ships.

Sec. 186.—Nothing in the Army Act is to affect the application of the Naval Discipline Act, or any "Order in Council" made thereunder, when troops are embarked on board Her Majesty's ships.

LECTURE IV.

THE ARMY ACT—MISCELLANEOUS.

Execution of Sentence.

Sec. 57.—After the sentence of a court-martial has been confirmed, the following authorities have power to mitigate, remit, or commute it, namely :—The Queen, the commander-in-chief, the officer commanding the district or station where the prisoner is, or any prescribed officer, the commander-in-chief of India, or of an Indian Presidency, and the commander of the forces in a Colony.

Secs. 58-62.—Penal servitude sentences at home are to be undergone in a penal servitude prison. If a penal servitude sentence is passed in India, or in a Colony, or in a foreign country, the convict is to be sent home as soon as practicable to a penal servitude prison.

Secs. 63-66.—Sentences of imprisonment at home are to be undergone either in military custody or in a public prison; in India, or a Colony, or a foreign country, in military custody or in an authorised prison; prisoners may be sent home but not abroad to a prison.

Sec. 131.—A prisoner sentenced in India, or in a Colony, to over twelve months' imprisonment or to penal servitude, is to be transferred as soon as practicable to a prison or convict establishment at home, unless, in the case of imprisonment, the court or the Secretary of State shall for special reasons order otherwise.

Stolen Property.

Sec. 75.—Any stolen property, or goods taken in exchange for stolen property, found in possession of an offender convicted of theft, by court-martial, may be ordered by the confirming officer, or by the commander-in-chief, to be restored to the lawful owner; if the stolen property has been pawned or sold by the prisoner, it is, if recovered, to be restored to the lawful owner, but the person who bought it may be repaid for it out of any money found on the prisoner, by order of the confirming officer, or of the commander-in-chief.

Tolls.

Sec. 143.—Officers and soldiers of the Regulars on duty, or on the march, and also their horses, baggage, and prisoners are exempt from paying tolls, on roads, or at landing places, or bridges, but their boats, &c., on canals are not exempt; at ferries in Scotland, they are to pay half-price, and are to be taken over first if they so desire.

Civil Process.

Sec. 144.—A soldier cannot be taken out of the Army by any civil process, or compelled to appear in person before a court of law, except on account of a crime, or of a debt exceeding 30*l*.

Court of Request.

Sec. 148-150.—Military courts of requests composed of officers, may be held in India, in places beyond the jurisdiction of "Courts of Small Causes," for the recovery by civilian creditors, from officers and soldiers, of debts not exceeding 400 rupees; courts of requests may be convened by the officer commanding the camp, garrison, or post. The President must not be below the rank of captain; the members must each have five years' service. The

President, members, and witnesses must be sworn. If the court is satisfied as to the justness of the creditor's claim, it may award execution, and the debtor's property may be seized and sold by auction if necessary (but not his arms and equipment), and half of his pay may be stopped, if necessary, to liquidate the debt.

Jurisdiction.

Sec. 157.—No person subject to military law, who has been acquitted or convicted by court-martial, can be tried again by court-martial for the same offence.

Sec. 158.—No person who ceases to be subject to military law shall, except for mutiny, desertion, or fraudulent enlistment, be liable to be tried after three months for offences committed whilst he was subject to military law.

Sec. 159.—Any person subject to military law who commits an offence at one place may be tried for it at any other place, provided it is within the jurisdiction of an officer authorised to convene general courts-martial.

Sec. 160.—If a person is tried at one place for an offence committed elsewhere, his punishment is not to be greater than it would have been if tried at the place where the offence was committed.

Sec. 161.—After the expiration of three years, an offender cannot be tried for any previous offence, except mutiny, desertion, and fraudulent enlistment. And a soldier, after three years' exemplary service, cannot be tried for any offence previous to his three years' exemplary service, except mutiny and desertion on active service.

Sec. 162.—If a person, after being sentenced by a court-martial, is tried again for the same offence by a civil court, the military sentence must be taken into consideration. If a person is acquitted or convicted by the civil power for an offence, he cannot be tried under military law for that offence.

Legal Proceedings.

Sec. 166.—Any proceedings taken before a court of summary jurisdiction, in pursuance of this Act, shall be taken in accordance with the Summary Jurisdiction Act.

Sec. 167.—All fines, in default of payment, and all orders made under this Act, may be enforced by a term of imprisonment not exceeding three months.

Sec. 168.—All offences which may be prosecuted, and all fines which may be recovered under this Act, may be prosecuted and recovered in the Isle of Man, the Channel Islands, India, and the Colonies, in such courts and in such manner as may be provided by law.

LECTURE V.

The Army Act—Enlistment.

Sec. 76.—A person may be enlisted for twelve years, or for such less period as may be permitted, but not for more.

Sec. 77.—Enlistment may be either for the whole term in Army service, or for part of the term in Army service and the remainder in the Reserve.

Sec. 78.—A Secretary of State may from time to time vary the conditions of a soldier's service and permit him to

1. Enter the Reserve at once, and serve out the rest of his term in it.

2. Extend his Army service for a part or the whole of the unexpired portion of his term.

3. Extend the term of his enlistment up to twelve years.

4. Re-enter the Army from the Reserve for a part or the whole of the unexpired term of his enlistment, or to make up twelve years from date of enlistment.

Sec. 79.—Service towards discharge commences from date of attestation. All previous service is forfeited on conviction, or confession of desertion or fraudulent enlistment, and then service towards discharge commences from date of conviction, or date of order dispensing with trial.

A Secretary of State may restore such forfeited service if he thinks fit.

Sec. 80.—A person wishing to enlist receives a notice from a recruiting-sergeant to appear before a justice of the peace, in whose presence he answers the questions in the attestation paper, signs the paper, and takes the oath of allegiance; he is then said to be attested, begins to count service, and becomes subject to military law.

Sec. 81. A recruit is entitled to purchase his discharge within three months of his attestation by a payment of 10*l.*, unless at that time the Reserves are called out by proclamation, in which case he must continue to serve as long as the Reserves are serving.

Sec. 82. Recruits may be enlisted either for service in particular corps, or for general service. A soldier, when once appointed to a corps, shall complete his Army service in it, unless transferred under the following conditions :—

1. If enlisted for general service, he may at any time during his first three months' service be transferred to any corps of the same arm or branch.

2. With his own consent he may at any time be transferred.

3. If transferred to a corps in a different arm or branch, the conditions of his service may be altered so as to correspond with those of his new corps.

4. A soldier may be transferred to a corps of the same branch on home service, if he has been

invalided from abroad, or if he is medically unfit to go abroad with his corps, or if his corps goes abroad within two years of his completing his Army service.

5. A soldier on foreign service, if he has more than two years' Army service unexpired at the date of his corps leaving a foreign station, may, if he has Reserve service to put in, be transferred to any corps of the same branch on foreign service.

6. If a soldier has been transferred to serve either as a warrant-officer or in any corps, not infantry, cavalry, artillery, or engineers, he may be removed or transferred to any corps serving at home, or if he is abroad, to any corps serving on that station, or to his original corps, either in the rank he holds or any lower rank.

7. If a soldier has been guilty of desertion or fraudulent enlistment, or has been sentenced by a court-martial to six months' imprisonment for any offence, he becomes liable, partly or wholly in commutation of other punishment, to general service, and may be transferred to any corps of the Regular forces.

8. A soldier delivered into military custody, or committed by a court of summary jurisdiction as a deserter, becomes liable to transfer to any corps, and to serve in it without prejudice to his subsequent trial and punishment.

Sec. 84.—Subject to regulations made from time to time by a Secretary of State, a soldier, if in Army service, may, within three years of completing his original term of enlistment, be allowed to re-engage to make up twenty-one years' Army service.

Sec. 87.—Either in time of war, or when a soldier is on foreign service, or when the Reserves are called out by proclamation, the competent military authority may order the prolongation of a soldier's Army service, not exceeding twelve months.

Sec. 88.—In case of imminent national danger, Her Majesty may continue soldiers in Army service instead of transferring them in the usual course to the Reserve, and may call out the Reserves for permanent service.

Sec. 90.—Save as otherwise provided, every soldier, on completing his term of enlistment or re-engagement, shall be discharged as quickly as possible, and if abroad at the time, he may, if he wishes it, be sent home to be discharged.

And every soldier, on completing his Army service shall, if he has Reserve service to put in, be transferred to the Reserve, and if abroad at the time, shall be sent home as quickly as possible to be so transferred.

Sec. 98.—The penalty for unlawful recruiting is a fine of 50*l*.

Sec. 99.—The penalty for making a false answer to any question in the attestation paper is three months' imprisonment by civil power. If attested as a soldier, the offender may be dealt with either by civil power or by court-martial.

Sec. 100.—After three months' service and pay, a soldier cannot claim his discharge on account of error or illegality in his enlistment or re-engagement.

Sec. 101.—As regards enlistment, competent military authority means the commander-in-chief or adjutant-general, or any officer prescribed in that behalf; and Reserve means the 1st Class Army Reserve.

LECTURE VI.

THE ARMY ACT—BILLETING, AND IMPRESSMENT OF CARRIAGES.

Sec. 102.—The following sections contain the law as to billeting, any other law relating to billeting is hereby suspended.

Sec. 103.—Constables when duly required, and on the production of the route, shall provide billets for officers and soldiers and their horses.

Sec. 104.—Inns, hotels, livery stables, and retail wine-shops are considered "victualling houses," and are therefore liable to provide billets.

Sec. 105.—Officers and soldiers of the Regulars and their horses, if entitled to forage are entitled to billets.

Sec. 106.—The accommodation in billets consists of lodging and attendance for officer, lodging, attendance and food for soldier, and stable room and forage for horse. The prices are those authorised annually by Parliament (*vide* Schedule, Annual Act).

Sec. 107.—The police annually make a list of keepers of victualling houses liable to billets, and it is open to the inspection of persons interested.

Sec. 108.—No billets shall be ordered in excess of the number of officers, soldiers, and horses. The billets shall be handed to the officer or non-commissioned officer who demanded them, or to some duly authorised officer.

Complaints of victualling-house keepers are to be made to justices of the peace.

A constable may provide billets in a town, and within one mile of it. Justices of the peace may, if requested, direct billets to be given at other places besides those named on the route, and may require constables to furnish in writing the particulars of the billets they provided.

Sec. 109.—If a constable fails to do his duty, or if he is guilty of an offence relating to billets, he is liable to a fine of 10*l.*

Sec. 110.—If a victualling-house keeper refuses billets, or if he commits an offence relating to billets, he is liable to a fine of 5*l.*

Sec. 111.—If an officer or soldier commits an offence relating to billets, he is liable to a fine of 50*l.*

Impressment of Carriages.

Sec. 112.—Justices of the peace shall if duly requested, and on the production of the route, order constables to provide carriages, horses, and drivers for the conveyance of regimental baggage and stores; and persons having suitable carriages and horses shall furnish them on the constable's demand.

Sec. 113.—Schedule 3 contains the rate of payment for carriages and horses, and regulations concerning them. These rates may, if necessary, be increased by one-third by certain local authorities.

Sec. 114.—The police annually make a list of persons liable to furnish carriages and horses, and it is open to the inspection of persons interested.

Requisition of Emergency.

Sec. 115.—The Queen and the Lord Lieutenant of Ireland may, in cases of emergency, authorise general or field officers commanding Her Majesty's forces, to obtain carriages, horses, vessels, boats, &c., by a "Requisition of Emergency," but due payment is to be made.

Sec. 116.—If a constable fails to do his duty, or if he is guilty of an offence relating to impressment of carriages, he is liable to a fine of 20*l*.

Sec. 117.—If a person ordered by a constable to furnish carriages, horses, &c., refuses, or if he is guilty of an offence relating to impressment of carriages, he is liable to a fine of 10*l*.

Sec. 118.—If an officer or soldier is guilty of an offence relating to impressment of carriages, he is liable to a fine of 50*l*.

LECTURE VII.

FORFEITURE OF PAY, DEFERRED PAY, ETC., BY ROYAL WARRANT.

IN accordance with the terms of the Royal Warrant 1882, pay, deferred pay, good-conduct pay, service towards pension, and medals, decorations, annuities, and gratuities, are forfeited under the following circumstances:

Forfeiture of Pay.

Art. 766.—Pay is forfeited for every day of desertion or absence without leave over five days, or less than five days if convicted by court-martial of such offence; also for every day's imprisonment by civil power, court-martial, or commanding officer, or awaiting trial if afterwards convicted by civil court or court-martial, or under detention for absence if afterwards awarded imprisonment for it by commanding officer, or under detention after confessing desertion or fraudulent enlistment; also for the days in hospital caused by an offence.

If a commanding officer disposes summarily of a

Art. 767.—A soldier is to receive no pay on the day he is released from prison, neither is a non-commissioned officer to receive pay on the day he is reduced to the ranks.

Art. 768.—Soldiers acquitted, or illegally convicted, or released without trial (unless for confessing desertion or fradulent enlistment), are to get full pay from the date of their confinement, but must pay for their subsistence.

Art. 769.—Soldiers sent home from abroad as prisoners, for discharge, are to get no pay either whilst awaiting embarkation or during the voyage.

Art. 770.—A soldier is not entitled to pay when a prisoner of war, but the Secretary of State may restore his pay if the inquiry is satisfactory.

Art. 771.—If a commanding officer stops a soldier's liquor ration on board ship, the soldier forfeits 1d. a day. If the soldier is not drawing his liquor ration he nevertheless forfeits 1d. a day.

Forfeiture of Deferred Pay.

Art. 649.—Deferred pay is forfeited for every day on which service towards pension is forfeited.

Art. 650.—A general court-martial or a district court-martial may forfeit all or part of deferred pay already earned, but shall not award such forfeiture if the conviction does of itself entail it.

Art. 652c.—Deferred pay shall not be issued to a man sentenced by court-martial to be discharged with ignominy, or to a man discharged either as a bad character, or for giving a false answer on attestation, or for conviction by civil power, or on being sentenced to penal servitude.

Forfeiture of Good Conduct Pay.

Art. 927.—One badge is forfeited for each entry in the Regimental Defaulters' Book.

Art. 928.—The forfeiture of a badge includes the loss of any portion of a half-term of good conduct already given towards the restoration of a badge previously forfeited.

Art. 929.—A general court-martial or a district court-martial may forfeit one or more badges, but not if the conviction does of itself entail such forfeiture.

Art. 930.—All good-conduct badges are forfeited for an entry in the Regimental Defaulters' Book of improper enlistment whilst belonging to the Reserve, or on being sentenced to more than six months' imprisonment by civil power.

Art. 931.—All good-conduct badges are forfeited for an entry in the Regimental Defaulters' Book of an offence punishable by forfeiture of service towards limited engagement.

Art. 932.—All good-conduct badges are forfeited when sentenced by court-martial to be discharged with ignominy; or when discharged either as a bad character, or on conviction by civil power, or on being sentenced to penal servitude, or for giving a false answer on attestation.

Forfeiture of Service towards Pension.

Art. 580.—All service towards pension is forfeited when sentenced by court-martial to be discharged with ignominy: or when sentenced to be discharged either as a bad character, or on conviction by civil power, or on being sentenced to penal servitude, or for giving a false answer on attestation.

Art. 583.—A general court-martial or a district court-martial may forfeit part or the whole of past service towards pension, but not if the conviction does of itself entail such forfeiture.

Art. 583 I.—Service towards pension which has accrued or been forfeited under any previous warrant shall not be affected by this warrant.

Forfeiture of Medals, &c.

Art. 910.—All medals, decorations, annuities, and gratuities, are forfeited on conviction by court-martial of desertion, fraudulent enlistment, or of any offence under sections 17 and 18 Army Act, also when sentenced by court-martial to penal servitude, or discharged with ignominy.

Art. 911.—All medals, annuities, and gratuities are forfeited if trial for desertion or fraudulent enlistment is dispensed with; or if a soldier is discharged either for misconduct, or on conviction by civil power, or for being sentenced to penal servitude, or for giving a false answer on attestation; also if a soldier is sentenced to more than six months' imprisonment by civil power.

Art. 912.—A general court-martial or a district court-martial may forfeit any medals, decorations, annuities, and gratuities, but not if the offence does of itself entail such forfeiture.

Art. 913.—Forfeited medals, decorations, annuities, and gratuities may be restored by the Secretary of State on the recommendation of the commander-in-chief.

LECTURE VIII.

THE RULES OF PROCEDURE.

Courts-Martial.

Rule 13.—A prisoner, previous to his trial, is to be afforded proper opportunity of preparing his defence, and is to be allowed free communication with his witnesses, and with any friend or legal adviser he may wish to consult.

Rule 58.—The President is responsible that the trial is conducted properly, and in accordance with the Army Act, and that the prisoner has a fair trial, and does not suffer any disadvantage from ignorance, incapacity, or otherwise.

Rule 59.—It is the duty of the prosecutor to assist the court in administering justice, to behave impartially, to bring the whole transaction before the court, and not to take any unfair advantage of, or suppress evidence in favour of, the prisoner.

Rule 102.—If the convening officer, or the senior officer on the spot, considers it impossible, or inexpedient, to observe Rules 5, 8, 13, and 14, he may write a declaration to that effect, giving his reasons, and the trial may then take place and be as valid as if the above rules had been observed.

Duties of Judge-Advocate.

Rules 99–101.—The Judge-Advocate is to be appointed by the convening officer. There must always be a Judge-Advocate on a general court-martial, and in exceptional cases, there may be one on a district court-martial, if the convening officer is authorised to appoint one.

Disqualification for sitting on a court-martial is also disqualification for acting as Judge-Advocate.

The duties of a Judge-Advocate are to represent the Judge-Advocate General; to give his opinion on questions of law, to either the court, the prosecutor, or the prisoner; to inform the convening officer and the court of any informality or irregularity in the proceedings. At the conclusion of the case he will if necessary sum up the evidence, and give his opinion on the legal bearing of the case, before the court proceeds to consider their finding. Upon any point of law the court should be guided by his opinion. The judge-advocate must watch the interests of the prisoner, and maintain an entirely impartial position.

Courts of Inquiry.

Rule 123.—This rule does not apply to a court of inquiry on illegal absence, held under sec. 72 of the Army Act.

A court of inquiry may be assembled by the officer in command of any body of troops, and may be composed of any number of officers of any rank, and will be guided by the written instructions of the officer who assembles it. It has no judicial power, but has merely to collect evidence.

If the inquiry effects the character of an officer or soldier, opportunity must be given to him to be present, and to make any statement, and cross-examine witnesses, and produce witnesses. It cannot compel witnesses to attend, and cannot take evidence on oath. It will give no opinion on the conduct of an officer or soldier, and its proceedings cannot be given in evidence at a trial.

The proceedings are forwarded by the president to the officer who assembled the court of inquiry, in order that he may form his opinion, which, if adverse to the character of an officer or soldier, must be communicated to him. The court may be reassembled as often as necessary. Its members are not to be detailed to sit on any court-martial which may ensue.

LECTURE IX.

THE RULES OF EVIDENCE.

THE word evidence includes all legal means, exclusive of mere argument, which tend to prove or disprove any matter of fact, the truth of which is under investigation. The word proof means the effect of evidence.

The rules of evidence to be followed by courts-martial are to be those adopted in English courts of law.

Witnesses.—As a general rule, every person is competent to give evidence as a witness, the principal exceptions being prisoners jointly arraigned, for or against each other; husband and wife, for or against each other; a prisoner on his trial, for or against himself; also in the case of want of reason, or understanding, or ignorance of the nature of an oath, or of a very young child. A member of a court-martial is incompetent to give evidence for the prosecution. If a witness is proved to be incompetent he cannot give evidence at all; but should a witness be considered by the court to be incredible, his evidence will be recorded, but treated as valueless. As regards the incredibility of a witness, cross-examination and evidence as to character will test this; the evidence of a criminal or person of notorious bad character cannot be rejected, but should be received with caution.

Examination of Witnesses.— A witness is to be examined by the party calling him, cross-examined by the opposite party, and may be re-examined by the party calling him, but the re-examination must be confined to matters arising out of the cross-examination.

The court may at any time before the "finding" recall a witness, or call a fresh witness to clear up an obscure or doubtful point, but neither the prosecutor nor the prisoner can claim this as a right.

Satisfactory Evidence. — Satisfactory evidence is that amount of proof which satisfies an unprejudiced mind beyond all reasonable doubt. As a rule, the evidence of one credible witness is sufficient in point of law, except in cases of perjury, treason, and treason felony. The evidence of a single accomplice is sufficient, but it should be received with great caution. It is usual, however, to have two witnesses in all cases.

Rejection of Evidence.—The rejection of evidence tendered by a prisoner, or undue restriction of a prisoner in cross-examination, would be illegal; but if a prisoner asked for an adjournment so as to secure the attendance of witnesses who could not appear without serious expense or inconvenience, the court would have to elicit from the prisoner the nature of the evidence such witnesses would probably give, and might then either refuse or grant the request; but if they refuse they must record on the proceedings the request, the refusal, and the reason for the refusal.

Opinion of Witnesses.—The general opinion of a witness (unless he is an expert) is not evidence.

Privileges of Witnesses.—A witness is not to be compelled to criminate himself, but this privilege does not extend to answers showing civil liability. Official communications upon public affairs, confidential reports, and the minutes of a court of inquiry are privileged. Legal advisers are privileged; but medical men and clergymen are not privileged from disclosing professional communications.

Evidence as to Character.—Evidence as to character is given by the prosecutor after the finding, to assist the court in awarding punishment; it must not be given as evidence of guilt, but the prosecutor might give it to rebut evidence given on behalf of the prisoner. The prisoner may call witnesses to speak generally as to his character.

General Rules of Evidence.—There are five general rules of evidence, namely—

1. The best evidence obtainable must be produced.
2. Hearsay is not evidence.

3. The evidence must be confined to the point at issue.

4. The point at issue must be proved by the person who asserts the affirmative.

5. It is sufficient to prove the substance of the charge.

There are two presumptions in law, namely—

1. Every man is presumed to intend the necessary consequences of his own action.

2. Every man is presumed to be innocent until proved guilty.

Hearsay Evidence.—As regards Rule 2, hearsay is excluded because the statement was not made on oath, and the person affected by the statement had no opportunity of cross-examining the author. But there are two exceptions, first, in the case of certain dying declarations; second, statements forming part of what is known by the name of the "res gestæ," that is to say, of the fact forming the subject of inquiry. For example, the declaration of persons robbed, assaulted, &c., made immediately afterwards.

Burden of Proof.—As regards Rule 4, the prosecution must give evidence of the commission of the crime, after which the prisoner is bound to prove any facts from which he wishes the court to infer his innocence.

Special Finding.—As regards Rule 5, if the court thinks that the facts proved differ materially from the facts alleged in the charge, it is empowered by

Rule of Procedure 43, to record a special finding instead of a finding of Not Guilty.

Evidence may either be direct, circumstantial, or documentary.

Direct Evidence.—Direct evidence is that given from actual and personal knowledge of the fact charged.

Presumptive Evidence.—Presumptive evidence is that which affords proof from which the fact can be inferred. A well-established chain of incidents often carries with it a clearer conviction to the mind than direct evidence.

Documentary Evidence.—As regards documents, they may be either public or private, originals or copies, but Rule 1 must apply to them, namely, that the best possible evidence obtainable must be produced; public are preferable to private documents, and originals are preferable to copies.

The documents made evidence by the Army Act are specified in sec. 72, and secs. 163-165, Army Act, and consist of:—1. The record of declaration of a court of inquiry on illegal absence. 2. Attestations. 3. Records of service. 4. Anything published by authority, such as Queen's regulations, royal warrants, army circulars, army lists and gazettes. 5. Certified copies of entries in the regimental books. 6. Descriptive returns. 7. Certificate of civil convictions. 8. Proceedings and copies of proceedings of courts-martial.

True copies of documents must be certified as such by the person in charge of the originals.

Primary and Secondary Documentary Evidence.— Primary evidence of a document is given by producing the document for the inspection of the court. Secondary evidence of a private document is usually given by producing a copy and calling a witness to prove it to be correct, or by calling a witness who has seen the document and can give an account of its contents.

Handwriting.—Handwriting should be proved by the writer, or by some one well acquainted with the writing, or by an expert.

Conspirators.—When men are proved to have been acting in concert, for any illegal purpose such as conspiracy, mutiny, or sedition, the acts and statements of one of them may be given in evidence against the others, because they form part of the transaction to which the inquiry relates.

Admissions and Confessions.—Admissions as to collateral or comparatively unimportant facts are received by courts-martial. Voluntary confessions are received as evidence, but only against the person who makes them; but a confession made by one accomplice in the presence of another, if it implicates the latter, and is not contradicted at the time, would be evidence against the latter.

Depositions.—Depositions are not received as a general rule, but there are a few exceptions in the case of dangerous illness, &c. And then they should be taken on oath, before a magistrate in the presence of the prisoner, and signed by the deponent and the magistrate.

Dying Declarations.—Dying declarations are not received as a general rule, but would sometimes be received in the case of homicide, since it is supposed that the approach of death is a guarantee for truth.

LECTURE X.

THE MILITIA ACT.

Training.

Sec. 14.—Every Militiaman shall attend, at such place and time within the United Kingdom as may be prescribed, for "*preliminary training,*" not exceeding six months, and may be trained by officers and non-commissioned officers of the Regulars and Militia. This preliminary training shall not be included in the time of the "annual training."

Sec. 15.—Militia officers, or Militiamen, may with their own consent be called up for the purpose of instruction.

Sec. 16.—The *annual training* shall not be less than twenty-one nor more than twenty-eight days a year, and shall be at such place and time, within the United Kingdom, as may be prescribed.

Sec. 17.—Her Majesty in Council may order the annual training in any year to be extended to fifty-six days, or to be reduced below twenty-one days, or to be dispensed with altogether.

Embodiment.

Sec. 18.—In case of *imminent national danger* or great emergency, Her Majesty in Council, and by proclamation, may order the Militia to be *embodied*, and may order the Secretary of State to give the necessary directions, and such proclamation and directions shall be obeyed as if enacted in this Act.

Sec. 19.—If Parliament is not sitting at the time the Militia is ordered to be embodied, it shall be reassembled by proclamation within ten days.

Sec. 20.—It shall be lawful for Her Majesty, by proclamation, to order the Militia to be disembodied, and thereupon the Secretary of State shall give the necessary directions.

Desertion and Fraudulent Enlistment.

Sec. 23.—Any Militiaman who fails, without reasonable excuse, to appear at the time and place appointed either for preliminary or annual training, or for embodiment, shall be guilty in the case of embodiment either of desertion under sec. 12, Army Act, or of absence without leave under sec. 15,

Army Act, and in any other case of absence without leave under sec. 15, Army Act, and shall if he commits an offence under this section, or under secs. 12 & 15, Army Act, be liable, whether subject to military law or not, either to be tried and punished by court-martial, or to be convicted by civil power, and fined not less than 40s. and not more than 25l., and in default, imprisonment.

Sec. 24.—Sec. 154, Army Act, shall apply to a Militiaman who is a deserter, or absentee without leave, in the same manner as if he were in the Army, and any person falsely representing himself as a deserter or absentee from the Militia, shall be liable on conviction by civil power to three months' imprisonment.

Sec. 25.—The punishment for inducing or assisting a Militiaman to desert, or absent himself, is a fine by civil power not exceeding 20l.

Sec. 26.—If a Militiaman unlawfully enlists into the Auxiliary, or Reserve forces, or Royal Navy; or if a man of the Reserve forces, or of the Auxiliary forces other than Militia, or of the Royal Navy, unlawfully enlists into the Militia, such person, if on service as part of the Regulars at the time he commits the offence, shall be guilty of fraudulent enlistment, and in any other case shall be guilty of making a false answer; and shall, whether subject to military law or not, be liable either to be tried under sec. 13 or 33, Army Act, or to be convicted by civil power and sentenced to imprisonment not exceeding three months, or to a fine not exceeding 25*l.* for a first offence, and to imprisonment not exceeding six months for a subsequent offence.

The punishment for attempting to commit an offence under this section is imprisonment by court-martial, and half the above fine or imprisonment if convicted by civil power.

Sec. 27.—Any Militiaman who is committed as a deserter or absentee, or convicted of desertion, fraudulent enlistment, or absence without leave, or who is dealt with summarily by his commanding officer for such offences, shall, in addition to his other punishment, be liable to a certain amount of further service.

Sec. 28.—If a Militiaman illegally absents himself whilst he is subject to military law, a court of inquiry may be assembled after twenty-one days, under sec. 72, Army Act; and if a Militiaman fails to appear for preliminary or annual training, or embodiment, and his absence continues for fourteen days, his commanding officer shall make an entry in the regimental books of his absence, and this entry shall be conclusive evidence of the fact of such absence.

Trial and Punishment.

Sec. 43.—An alleged offender shall not be liable to be tried both by court-martial and by civil power for the same offence. A Militiaman may be tried by court-martial or by civil power, or dealt with by his commanding officer, after his Militia service has expired, for an offence committed before it expired, within two months after the offence becomes known to his commanding officer, if then apprehended, or within two months after his apprehension.

If a Militiaman has several times been guilty of desertion, fraudulent enlistment, or making a false answer, he may be deemed to belong to any one of the corps in question, and may be charged with any number of the above offences at the same time, and if found guilty may be punished as if previously convicted of any such offence.

LECTURE XI.

THE RESERVE FORCES ACT.

Army Reserve.

Sec. 3.—It shall be lawful for Her Majesty to keep up an Army Reserve, consisting of two classes. The strength of each class shall be decided upon by Parliament. Class 1 is liable for service either at home or abroad, and consists of two divisions. The second division is not liable to be called out until orders have been given to call out the whole of the first division. Class 2 is liable for service at home only, and consists of out-pensioners of Chelsea and Greenwich Hospitals, and of men who, having served in the Regulars for the full term of their original enlistment, enlist into the Army Reserve.

Calling out Army Reserve in Aid of the Civil Power.

Sec. 5.—The Secretary of State and the Lord Lieutenant of Ireland may, whenever they think necessary, call out the whole or part of the Army Reserve in aid of the civil power. And any officer commanding the troops in a town or district may, on the written requisition of a justice of the peace, call out the Army Reserve men of that town or district for the same purpose.

Punishment of Offences committed by Army Reserve.

Sec. 6.—An Army Reserve man who on two consecutive occasions fails to comply with the orders respecting payment, or who fails to attend at any place he is ordered to attend, or who uses threatening or insulting language to his superiors in the execution of their office, or who obtains pay by fraudulent means, or who fails to comply with orders or regulations under this Act, shall be guilty of an "*offence,*" and shall then, whether liable to military law or not, be liable either to be tried and punished by court-martial with imprisonment, or to be convicted by a court of summary jurisdiction, and fined not less than 40s., and not more than 25l.

If an Army Reserve man commits an offence under this section, or under sub-sections 2 and 3, sec. 142, Army Act, in presence of an officer, that officer may order him to be taken into either military or civil custody. A paymaster's certificate shall be proof of a failure to attend for pay, and the certificate of the officer or person before whom the Army Reserve man failed to appear shall be proof of a failure to attend.

Militia Reserve.

Secs. 8 and 9.—It shall be lawful for Her Majesty to keep up a Militia Reserve, the strength of which shall be decided upon by Parliament. Every man enlisted into the Militia Reserve shall either be enlisted for six years, or for the residue of his Militia engagement.

Annual training of Reserves.

Sec. 11.—All men of the Army Reserve and Militia Reserve may be called out for annual training at such times and places within the United Kingdom as may be prescribed, not exceeding twelve days a year for an Army Reserve man, and fifty-six days a year for a Militia Reserve man, and when called out may be attached to and trained with the Regular or the Auxiliary forces. But the annual training of the

Militia Reserve man shall be instead of the annual training to which he is liable as a Militiaman.

Permanent Service of Reserves.

Secs. 12 and 13.—In case of imminent national danger or great emergency, Her Majesty in Council, and by proclamation, may call out the Army and Militia Reserves on permanent service, and may order a Secretary of State to give the necessary directions; and the proclamation and directions shall be obeyed as if enacted in this Act, and after that time the Reserves shall be deemed to be on permanent service. If Parliament is not sitting at the time, it shall be reassembled within ten days.

Punishment for non-attendance when called out.

Sec. 15.—When an Army Reserve or Militia Reserve man is called out for annual training, or on permanent service, or when an Army Reserve man is called out in aid of the civil power, and such man fails to appear, he shall, if called out on permanent service or in aid of the civil power, be guilty of desertion or of absence without leave; and if called out for annual training, be guilty of absence without leave. And any Army Reserve or Militia Reserve man who commits an offence under this section, or under secs. 12 and 15, Army Act, shall be liable, whether subject to military law or not at the time, to be tried and punished by court-martial or by the civil power, in which latter case the punishment is to be a fine of from 40s. to 25l., and in default, imprisonment.

Deserters and Absentees.

Sec. 16.—Sec. 154, Army Act, shall apply to a deserter or absentee without leave from the Army Reserve or Militia Reserve, in like manner as it applies to a deserter from the Army. And if the man is delivered into military custody, or committed, he may be tried and punished as prescribed by this Act.

Any person falsely representing himself as a deserter or absentee without leave from the Army Reserve or Militia Reserve, shall, on conviction by the civil power, be liable to three months' imprisonment with hard labour.

MILITARY TOPOGRAPHY.

Definitions.—A "bearing" is the direction of an object with reference to the magnetic meridian. A "check-bearing" is a bearing taken to test the accuracy of a point already fixed. Bearings taken from points already fixed, to fix the position of other points, are termed "cross-bearings." A "contour" is the line of intersection of a hill by a horizontal plane. "Interpolation" means finding your own position by taking bearings from it to two fixed points, and protracting the opposite bearings from those points. The "datum level" is the level with which all other heights are compared; the sea-level at high water is taken as the datum level for the Ordnance maps. The "crest line" is the line showing the shape of the top of a hill. "Under-features" are minor features springing from main features. A "knoll" is a small eminence. A "spur" is a prominent feature projecting from high ground. A "watershed" means the line defining the highest part of a feature or chain of hills. A "plateau" is a flat surface on top of a hill. A "basin" is a level surrounded or nearly surrounded by hills. A "ravine" is a narrow valley with steep sides. A "col" is a neck or saddle connecting adjacent heights.

Meridian.—A "meridian" is the arc joining the poles of the earth through the station of an observer. The direction of the true north can be found approximately by an observation of the north star, or of the shadow of a stick planted vertically in the ground at noon. The magnetic needle does not point to the true north, but varies in different parts of the world, and from year to year. In London previous to 1660 the variation was east of north. In 1660 there was no variation, and in 1882 it was 18° west of north in London and 22° west of north in the south of Ireland.

Horizontal Equivalents.—"Horizontal equivalents"

are terms used in contouring. They are the bases of right-angled triangles of fixed altitude, and with hypotenuses at certain degrees of slope. In other words, they are the horizontal distances between contours.

The formula for finding them is

$$\frac{19 \cdot 1 \times \text{vertical interval in feet}}{\text{degree of slope}} = \text{Horizontal equivalent in yards.}$$

Scale of Shade.—A "scale of shade" has been adopted for the sake of uniformity for slopes, varying from 2° to 35°; steep slopes being shaded dark and gentle slopes light. In hachuring dark shades are obtained by thick strokes close together, and light shades by thin strokes far apart. Slopes of 60° 30°, and 15° are considered inaccessible for infantry, cavalry, and artillery respectively.

Sections.—A "section" is the intersection of a hill by a vertical plane. In drawing sections on paper, heights are usually exaggerated, so as to convey the impression of sufficient elevation. For example, if the horizontal scale was 6 inches to a mile, the vertical scale would probably be 18 or 24 inches to a mile, or, in other words, heights to distances at 3 or 4 to 1. To draw a section from a contoured map, it is necessary to know the horizontal and vertical scales and the vertical intervals between contours.

Triangulation.—For a field sketch of one or two miles the length of base should be about a quarter, for larger sketches less. The bases for the survey of Great Britain were measured near Salisbury, Hounslow, and Lough Foyle, and were 7 or 8 miles long. The lines of a triangulation should intersect at as near right angles as possible; a very acute angle is not to be trusted. The base should be level, with an extensive view from it all round. On the first triangles laid down, others and much larger ones may be built up, and the work extended over a whole country or district if necessary. Check bearings should be taken from time to time to test the accuracy of the work.

Field Sketching.—A base line is first chosen, measured, and laid down on paper, and a triangulation made, embracing as many useful points as possible for future use (a level road may often be used as a base). The roads and boundaries should then be traversed by taking bearings and pacing the distances, and the detail, such as rivers, hedges, woods, marshes, houses, &c., put in. The crest lines of the hills should then be drawn, and contours at 10 or 20 feet vertical interval, according as the scale is 12 or 6 inches to a mile. The sketch can then be shaded, cleaned up and finished, and the scale and north point put in.

The various methods of finding points are by triangulation, offsets, interpolation, cross-bearings, and a directing line. Care should be taken to avoid the necessity of going over the ground more than once. Contours are drawn by standing on the crest line, and taking the slope of the hill with a clinometer, and then marking off the horizontal equivalents from the scale on the protractor.

TOPOGRAPHICAL RECONNAISSANCE.

A TOPOGRAPHICAL reconnaissance consists of a sketch and written report of the country, or of any portion of the country, such as a road, river, defensive position, ground suitable for camps, outposts, &c.

The sketch should be made first, and whilst it is being made, notes or memoranda should be made in a pocket-book from which the report can afterwards be drawn up. Much information for the report can be obtained by questioning the inhabitants.

The scale for a road or river sketch is usually 2 or 3 inches to a mile, and for the sketch of a position 6 inches to a mile. The reports should be on Army Forms if they are available, but if much pressed for time, notes may be made on the margin or back of the sketch instead.

Reconnaissance of a road.—The reconnaissance of a road can be conveniently made by an officer preceding the troops by at least one day's march, and sending back his work every evening by a mounted orderly. The sketch, if time permits, can be made by compass, the fields, woods, cross-roads, &c., being put in by eye, commanding heights within range of fire-arms being fixed by cross-bearings.

If without a compass or if pressed for time, an eye sketch should be made.

The report should describe the country, roadway, rivers, bridges, villages, water, fuel, supplies, halting-places, camping grounds, positions, branch roads, railways, &c.

Reconnaissance of a River.—The usual object of reconnoitring a river is to ascertain how a force may cross it, or may prevent the enemy from crossing it. The sketch should be made in the same way as a road sketch; the report should specify the breadth, depth, swiftness of current, and the liability to floods, to dry up and to freeze, the height and nature of the banks, the bridges and places suitable for bridges, the fords, ferries, tributaries, houses, and villages, the nature of the valley through which the river flows, and the means of crossing or preventing an enemy from crossing.

Reconnaissance of a Position.—A hilly country is best for a defensive position. The extent of a position should be proportioned to the strength of the force intended to hold it. The view should be extensive and uninterrupted, the ground suitable for the action of all three arms; it should not be commanded, and there should be some protection for the flanks.

For the defence of an average position, including

reserves, allow three infantry per yard, cavalry about one-tenth infantry, and three guns per 1000 infantry.

There are usually two lines, and the depth of the position should be sufficient to allow 600 yards between the two lines for manœuvring.

The sketch should be made either by compass or by eye-sketching on the scale of 6 inches to a mile. The report should describe the ground, and also the roads leading from and to the position, the number and distribution of the troops, the obstacles and the nature of the field-works, and entrenchments required to strengthen the position, the probable mode of attack and the proposed method of defence, and the means of effecting an advance or retreat.

Accommodation on a March.—To compute the population of a village the houses can be counted, and five persons allowed for a small and ten for a large house.

Accommodation on a march means half of every house, the other half being left for the inhabitants; every room with a fireplace is to be considered habitable.

The approximate available accommodation for troops can be found by allowing one man for each yard of front of each room, but for very wide rooms allow two or three men for each yard of front. For horses allow 6 feet by 9 feet for each horse. A small house may be put down for two and a large house for from ten to twenty horses.

Supplies.—To calculate hay. As a cubic yard weighs 200 lbs., let H = height, B = breadth, and L = length of the stack in yards; then H B L × 200 = the content of the stack in pounds.

If the stack is not rectangular, H must be measured from the ground to one-third of the roof, and B and L must be the mean breadth and the mean length respectively.

To compute grain. As a cubic yard contains $20\frac{1}{4}$ bushels, and as a bushel of oats weighs 42 lbs., and a bushel of wheat 62 lbs; the weight of oats = x cubic yards × $20\frac{1}{4}$ × 42, and the weight of wheat = x cubic yards × $20\frac{1}{4}$ × 62.

Water.—To find the swiftness of the current, throw a cork in the stream, and note the number of yards it travels in a minute. Multiplying by 60 gives the number of yards an hour, and reducing the yards to miles, 1 mile an hour is called sluggish, 2 ordinary, 3 rapid, 5 very rapid, and 6 a torrent.

To calculate the number of gallons of water, find the number of cubic feet, and multiply by $6\frac{1}{4}$. This gives the number of gallons.

Distance by Sound.—Sound travels 370 yards a second; therefore by noting the number of seconds between the flash or smoke of a gun and the report, and multiplying by 370, you obtain the distance, in yards.

MILITARY BRIDGES.

A BRIDGE is usually composed of piers, arches, and roadway. The piers support the arches, and the arches support the roadway.

In military bridges there are no arches; instead of them, strong beams of wood called baulks, or road-bearers, are laid from pier to pier and support the roadway.

Any bridge which can be carried with an army and can quickly be put together may be termed a military bridge. There are two kinds of military bridges, namely, "standing" and "floating" bridges. Troops may also be passed across a river by what are termed "flying bridges," or by ferries, if there are no fords.

Standing bridges include pile, trestle, frame, and ladder bridges.

Pile Bridges—A pile bridge is formed by driving several rows of stout piles into the bed of the river, the tops being sawn off level so as to receive the "cap plates;" each pier is then strengthened by braces, and on the cap plates the baulks are laid, and upon the baulks a roadway of planks.

These bridges are suitable for deep and muddy rivers not liable to sudden floods, and are very durable. Small piles may be driven in by hand with "mauls," but some kind of pile-driving machine is necessary for large piles.

Trestle Bridges.—Trestle bridges are suitable to shallow rivers which have sound beds and are not liable to sudden floods; they are very portable, and can be made of any kind of timber; they may be either two, three or four-legged, and are formed of legs, braces, ledgers, and transoms. The road bearers rest on the transoms and support a roadway of planks. Trestles may quickly be placed in position if the water is shallow enough to admit of placing them by hand, but if the water is too deep and there are no boats available, they may be slid into their places down an inclined plane made of two baulks.

There are four kinds of frame bridges, namely, single and double "lock," and single and treble "sling."

Single Lock Bridge.—The single lock bridge consists of two frames locking into each other at an angle not greater than 120 degrees. Each frame consists of two standards, a ledger, a transom, and two braces.

To construct a single lock bridge, footings should first be made for the two frames; the section of the chasm is then measured and marked out on the ground by tapes and pickets. The standards are then laid on the section and marked with chalk where the ledgers and transoms are to be lashed. One frame should be 18 inches wider than the other, in order that it may lock outside it, and each frame should be 1 foot wider at the butts than at the tips of the standards.

To make a frame: lay the two standards on the ground, at right angles to the chasm, nearly parallel to each other and as far apart as the intended width of roadway, their butts towards the chasm, and lash the ledger and transom to the standards at the points marked by chalk; the ledger above and the transom below. Then square the frames and lash the braces to the standards, two butts and one tip above and one tip below.

The frames as soon as they are completed are lowered by foot ropes until the butts of the standards rest on the footings, and are then gradually launched forward, by means of two fore and two back guys to each, until they lock into each other, the standards of each frame resting on the transom of the other. A transom is then laid on the fork, on which the road bearers rest, and the roadway is then made. This bridge is suitable for a span of 30 feet, and can be made by 2 non-commissioned officers and 20 sappers (half on each side of the chasm) in rather more than one hour.

Double Lock Bridge. — A double lock bridge consists of two frames similar to those of the single lock, but of equal width, locking into a connecting frame. There are two points of support above the chasm for the roadway, namely, one on each frame. This bridge is suitable for a span of 40 feet, and can be made by 2 non-commissioned officers and 30 sappers in about 3 hours.

Single Sling Bridge.—A single sling bridge is made of two frames locking into each other at least 9 feet above the roadway; from the locking point a centre transom is slung so that there are three points of support above the chasm, namely, one on each frame and one on the centre or swinging transom. This bridge is suitable for a span of 50 feet.

Treble Sling Bridge.—The treble sling bridge is similar to the single sling, but has three swinging transoms, so that there are five points of support above the chasm, namely, one on each frame and three on the slung or swinging transoms. This bridge is suitable for a span of 70 feet.

Ladder Bridge.—To make a double ladder bridge, a cart or gun limber is run into the stream with a ladder secured to it, the shafts are then raised vertically and secured by guy ropes to pickets on each bank, a second ladder is then passed to the other bank, and the ladders are secured to a beam lashed across the shafts of the cart; the roadway is formed by covering the rungs of the ladders with planks. This bridge is only suitable for infantry in single file. If the stream is wide, several carts and ladders may be used. Another method suitable to a channel not wider than the ladders, is to pass two ladders across the channel, and set them up on their edges, the earth being banked up over their ends so that they may remain steady, and then laying planking across them in the usual way.

Floating Bridges.

Floating bridges include boat and raft bridges, also pontoon and cask bridges.

Boat Bridges.—The boats should be of the same size, and will then be equally immersed by equal weights, and the roadway will be level; they will be more secure if covered with canvas; each boat should be moored stem and stern, and they should all be connected together by pieces of timber lashed across their ends, so as to keep the proper intervals and relieve the baulks from strain. The baulks are fastened to a saddle or trestle, fixed in each boat and rising above the gunwale. The chesses forming the roadway are lashed down upon the baulks in the usual manner, by ribands and rack lashings. The bridge will be more secure if the boats are allowed to undulate a little, but they should not dip or heel very much, for which reason the baulks are made to rest above instead of on the gunwales; the buoyancy of each boat should be such that the greatest weight will not bring the gunwales down less than one foot from the water.

Raft Bridges.—Rafts of light timber, such as fir and pine, make very good floating piers; their buoyancy, however, is not very great, and if long in the water they are apt to become waterlogged unless their ends are tarred. They take a long time, but are not difficult to make, and cannot be sunk. Each pier should be at least 45 feet long, and the timbers should be connected by braces. The up-stream end of a pier should be angular, so as to offer the least resistance to the current. The piers should be anchored and connected together like boats, and should also have saddles for the road bearers to rest on. The buoyancy of a raft may be increased by having more than one tier of logs.

Roadway of Bridges.—The roadway of military bridges is usually formed by laying baulks or beams of wood called road bearers, from pier to pier, and above them, and at right angles to them, planks or chesses.

The roadway is usually 8 or 9 feet wide in the clear, and is formed by laying five baulks (which should be strong in proportion to the weight they are required to support) parallel to each other and at equal distances apart; at each pier the road bearers should be either all butts or all tips, so that the planking may lie evenly upon them, and that there may be no sudden drop. If planks or chesses are used they are racked down in their places upon the baulks by ribands and rack lashings. The roadway should have a slight rise or camber towards the centre, as it is sure to yield there after heavy traffic, and it may be laid simultaneously from each bank of the river. If spars are used instead of planks or chesses, the inequalities must be filled up with brushwood, clay, &c. If the roadway is above the level of the ground, ramps or slopes of earth leading up to it are necessary. A handrail of rope on each side about three feet above the roadway is also necessary.

Flying Bridges and Ferries.—Flying bridges are sometimes formed by mooring a boat or other floating body in a river, so that the stream may act on it obliquely, and help to move it across the river.

A boat is moored by a rope or cable to a buoy in the centre of the stream, the rope being at least $1\frac{1}{2}$ times the breadth of the river; long narrow boats are best, as the current has a greater length of side to act upon and there is less resistance to the bow. If the stream is very wide two boats may be thus used, and so regulated as to meet in the stream, exchange ropes, and continue their passage across the river.

If the river is unfordable, and there is no time or means to make a bridge, a river may often be crossed by ferries. Boats, rafts, and pontoons are used for this purpose, and may either be rowed across, or may haul themselves across by means of a warp stretched from one bank to the other.

Fords.—Fords are discovered by questioning the inhabitants, observing where wheel-tracks enter and leave a river, by taking soundings from a boat with a rod, and by carefully examining the river where the banks are low. Rivers are more frequently fordable in a slanting direction than straight across. The following depths are fordable if the bed of the river is sound. For infantry 3 feet, for cavalry 4 feet, for artillery with ammunition boxes 2 feet 4 inches. Fords should be carefully marked by pickets driven into the bed of the river, the heads of the pickets being connected by a rope, and if the pickets are marked, a rise or fall of the water will be at once apparent.

www.ingramcontent.com/pod-product-compliance
Lightning Source LLC
Chambersburg PA
CBHW030244170426
43202CB00009B/615